Teaching Grammar in Second Language Classrooms

"This comprehensive and up-to-date book addresses the contentious topic of L2 grammar instruction. Unique in combining theory, research findings, and practical activities, it is written in a very accessible and reader-friendly style."

Neomy Storch, The University of Melbourne, Australia

" … an important effort to make SLA theory and research accessible for language teachers. Not only do Nassaji and Fotos provide clear and concise descriptions of current thought regarding the role of grammar and communication in the L2 classroom, they also present classroom activities that are supported by the latest research in SLA. Given the controversy surrounding grammar instruction, this book will provide teachers with practical, research-based information, enabling them to make informed decisions regarding their own classroom practices."

Shawn Loewen, Michigan State University, USA

Recent SLA research recognizes the necessity of attention to grammar and demonstrates that form-focused instruction is especially effective when it is incorporated into a meaningful communicative context. Designed specifically for second-language teachers, this text identifies and explores the various options for integrating a focus on grammar and a focus on communication in classroom contexts and offers concrete examples of teaching activities for each option. Each chapter includes a description of the option, its theoretical and empirical background, examples of activities illustrating in a non-technical manner how it can be implemented in the classroom, questions for reflection, and a list of useful resources that teachers can consult for further information.

Hossein Nassaji is Professor of Applied Linguistics in the Department of Linguistics at the University of Victoria, Canada.

Sandra Fotos, retired Professor of English and Applied Linguistics, Senshu University, Tokyo, Japan, is currently an adjunct at the University of Victoria, Canada.

ESL & Applied Linguistics Professional Series
Eli Hinkel, Series Editor

Visit **www.routledge.com/education** for additional information on titles in the ESL & Applied Linguistics Professional Series.

Teaching Grammar in Second Language Classrooms

Integrating Form-Focused Instruction in Communicative Context

Hossein Nassaji and Sandra Fotos

 Routledge
Taylor & Francis Group

NEW YORK AND LONDON

First published 2011
by Routledge
711 Third Avenue, New York, NY 10017

Simultaneously published in the UK
by Routledge
2 Park Square, Milton Park, Abingdon, Oxon OX14 4RN

Routledge is an imprint of the Taylor & Francis Group, an informa business

© 2011 Taylor & Francis

The right of Hossein Nassaji and Sandra Fotos to be identified as authors of this work has been asserted by them in accordance with sections 77 and 78 of the Copyright, Designs and Patents Act 1988.

Typeset in Minion by Integra Software Services Pvt. Ltd, Pondicherry, India
Printed and bound in the United States of America by
Edwards Brothers Malloy

Library of Congress Cataloging in Publication Data
Nassaji, Hossein.
Teaching grammar in second language classrooms: integrating form-focused instruction in communicative context / Hossein Nassaji and Sandra Fotos.
p. cm. – (ESL & applied linguistics professional series)
Includes bibliographical references and index.
1. Second language acquisition. 2. Grammar, Comparative and general – Study and teaching. 3. Language and languages – Study and teaching. I. Fotos, Sandra. II. Title.
P118.2.N37 2011
418.0071 – dc22
2010022099

ISBN 13: 978-0-415-80204-8 (hbk)
ISBN 13: 978-0-415-80205-5 (pbk)
ISBN 13: 978-0-203-85096-1 (ebk)

Contents

Preface

This book examines the most recent advances in theory and research on communicative grammar instruction and the various instructional options for implementing it effectively in second language (L2) classrooms. A consideration of L2 teaching over the past few decades reveals a fundamental shift in the teaching of grammar from one in which grammar instruction was central, to one in which grammar instruction was absent, and to the recent reconsideration of the significance of the role of grammar instruction.

For many years, language teaching was equated with grammar teaching. It was believed that language was mainly composed of grammar rules and that knowing those rules would be sufficient for learners to acquire the language. With the rise of communicative teaching approaches in the 1970s, the teaching of grammar was considered undesirable. Teachers were encouraged to believe that grammar instruction was old-fashioned, uninteresting, and best avoided. Researchers claimed that teaching grammar had little impact on learners' grammatical development and did not lead to the development of communicative competence; hence, it had to be eliminated from L2 classrooms (e.g., Krashen, 1981, 1985, 1993; Krashen & Terrell, 1983). Some even went so far as to argue that grammar teaching was not only unhelpful but was also detrimental. Prabhu (1987, p. 2), for example, in describing the impetus for his procedural task-based project, pointed out:

> Attempts to systematize input to the learners through a linguistically organized syllabus, or to maximize the practice of particular parts of language structure through activities deliberately planned for that purpose were regarded as being unhelpful and detrimental to the desired preoccupation with meaning in the classroom.

Recent research in second language acquisition (SLA), however, has led to a reconsideration of the importance of grammar. Many researchers now believe that grammar teaching should not be ignored in second language classrooms. Language teaching professionals have also become increasingly aware that grammar instruction plays an important role in language teaching and learning. There are a number of reasons for this re-evaluation of the role of grammar. First, the hypothesis that language can be learned without some degree of consciousness has been found to be theoretically problematic (e.g., Schmidt, 1993, 1995, 2001; Sharwood Smith, 1993). In addition, there is ample empirical evidence that teaching approaches that focus primarily on meaning with no focus on grammar are inadequate (Harley & Swain, 1984; Lapkin, Hart, & Swain, 1991; Swain, 1985). Third, recent SLA research has demonstrated that instructed language learning has major effects on both the rate and the ultimate level of L2 acquisition. In particular, research has shown that form-focused instruction is especially effective when it is incorporated into a meaningful communicative context. However, there are still many questions about how to teach grammar effectively, and in particular, how to integrate most effectively a focus on grammatical forms and a focus on meaningful communication in L2 classrooms. Richards (2002) has referred to this question as "the central dilemma," in language teaching.

Here the key questions from the perspective of teachers are: (1) how can grammar be brought back to L2 classrooms without returning to the traditional models of grammar teaching that have often been found to be ineffective? (2) how can a focus on grammar be combined with a focus on communication? (3) what are the different ways of integrating grammar instruction and communicative interaction? and (4) more importantly, how can the opportunity for focus on grammar be maximized without sacrificing opportunities for a focus on meaning and communication?

Current SLA theory and research have begun to examine these questions. The results, sometimes published in journal articles or book chapters, have led to a number of new insights. However, it seems that no matter what current research suggests about how to integrate grammar instruction and communicative language teaching, this has minimally affected L2 pedagogy. One major reason for this is that most of these publications are academic in style; thus, they are not easily accessible to teachers (R. Ellis, 1997).

The aim of this book is to pull this body of new knowledge together and make it accessible to teachers. We will: (1) examine recent advances in communicative focus on form and what they have to offer to language teachers; (2) identify and explore the various options for integrating a focus on grammar and a focus on communication in classroom contexts; and (3) offer concrete examples of activities for each option. There is no shortage of discussion of methodologies that focus on grammatical forms alone or those that provide opportunities for communication. However, there is a need to explore ideas, techniques, or procedures that originate in the most recent SLA theory and research. This book addresses this need. The aim is not to simply survey research findings in this area. Rather, it is to discuss, in a nontechnical manner, the insights and implications from this research and make them accessible to teachers in ways in which they can see their potential relevance.

We will begin with an overview of the changes in grammar instruction over the years, and then present six recent input- and output-based instructional options for teaching grammar communicatively, including processing instruction, textual enhancement, discourse-based grammar teaching, interactional feedback, grammar-focused tasks, and collaborative output tasks. Each chapter introduces one of these options, including a description of the option, its theoretical and empirical background, and examples of activities to illustrate how it can be implemented in the classroom, questions for reflection, and a list of useful materials. We will also discuss the role of context in teaching grammar, and its implications for how best to implement a communicative focus on grammar in different pedagogical settings. By drawing on our own experiences as second and foreign language teachers, teacher educators, and SLA researchers, our goal is, therefore, to explore not only options for effective grammar teaching practices but also the contextual factors, goals, and constraints that may impact their usefulness in L2 classrooms.

The Intended Audience of the Book

This book is intended for those who are interested in second language learning and its implications for second language teaching. It is particularly directed at teachers and teacher trainers who wish to explore the different ways in which a focus on grammar can be integrated into communicative lessons. Because the book explores recent developments in one of the key areas of L2 acquisition and their impact on language pedagogy, it will appeal to students in second and foreign language courses who do not have a background in SLA, but who remain interested in the relationships among theory, research and classroom practices. For the same reason, it will also appeal to L2 researchers and graduate students in the field of SLA who are interested in the role of form-focused instruction in L2 classroom acquisition. The book can be used in a variety of ways. It can be used as a classroom text in courses with a focus on different methods of teaching grammar, as a handbook for teachers, or as a supplementary resource along with other more theoretical textbooks on instructed SLA.

The Organization of the Book

The book consists of nine chapters organized into three main parts. Parts I and II examine input-based and output-based grammar teaching, and Part III discusses the role of context.

Chapter 1, entitled "The Changing View of Grammar Instruction," provides a brief overview of traditional and current approaches to grammar instruction. It also examines recent developments in communicative focus on form and their implications for instructing grammar in L2 classrooms.

Chapter 2, entitled "Focus on Grammar through Processing Instruction," explores how grammar can be taught through processing input or what has been called "processing instruction." The chapter describes this approach, reviews its theoretical and empirical underpinnings, and provides examples of activities to show how structured input and input-processing techniques can be used in classroom instruction.

Chapter 3, entitled "Focus on Grammar through Textual Enhancement," examines textual enhancement as a tool in grammar instruction. Textual enhancement is a technique that highlights certain textual features of input that might go unnoticed under normal circumstances. This can be achieved through physical manipulation of the text, such as underlining, bolding or providing numerous usages of the form in communicative input, or "flooding." The chapter discusses textual enhancement strategies, reviews research findings about their usefulness, and presents classroom activities.

Chapter 4, entitled "Focus on Grammar through Discourse," explores grammar teaching through the use of discourse. Successful language instruction requires that learners have extensive exposure to communicative language use in authentic contexts. Thus, recent pedagogy for grammar teaching often advocates a discourse-based approach where grammar instruction is supported by the provision of L2 discourse containing multiple instances of the instructed form. This chapter examines insights from research on the use of discourse-based approaches, particularly data-driven approaches, to support communicative grammar instruction.

Chapter 5, entitled "Focus on Grammar through Interactional Feedback," discusses how learners' attention can be drawn to form through interactional feedback. SLA researchers now widely agree that it is crucial for L2 instruction to provide learners with ample opportunities for meaningful interaction, and also to provide opportunities to receive feedback on their output. This chapter will consider how a focus on grammar can be achieved when learners are involved in meaningful interaction with the teacher or other learners. This chapter also provides examples of various interactional strategies that can be used to provide learners with opportunities for feedback on grammar.

Chapter 6, entitled "Focus on Grammar through Structured Grammar-Focused Tasks," explores how communicative tasks can be designed in ways that draw learners' attention to particular grammatical forms. The chapter reviews different grammar-focused tasks, such as structure-based tasks, problem-solving tasks, information exchange tasks, and interpretation tasks. It also demonstrates how opportunities can be created to engage learners actively in performing such tasks effectively in L2 classrooms.

Chapter 7, entitled "Focus on Grammar through Collaborative Output Tasks," discusses how a focus on grammar can be achieved through engaging learners in activities in which they attempt to produce language collaboratively. The chapter describes this option, examines the theories and research that support it, and presents examples of activities that can be used in the classroom.

Chapter 8, entitled "The Role of Context in Focus on Grammar," addresses issues arising from the differences between instructional contexts and their implications for how best to implement a communicative focus on grammar in these contexts. It is argued that effective grammar instruction should take into consideration variability in instructional contexts, at both the micro and macro levels. This chapter examines the role of pedagogical contexts in classroom teaching. The goal is to consider various contextual factors, such as those related to the differences between second and foreign language contexts (e.g., ESL vs. EFL), beginners and adult learners, age, and the teacher (native speaker versus non-native speaker as teacher) and their implications for effective grammar teaching. We suggest that activities should be designed in ways that are consistent with the goals of each context.

The final chapter, Chapter 9, is the concluding chapter. It summarizes the main points considered in the previous chapters and offers a number of additional remarks related to teaching and integrating grammar into L2 classrooms effectively.

Acknowledgments

We would like to thank Taylor Marie Young and Carrie Hill, two of our applied linguistics students at University of Victoria, for their diligent proof-reading of the text and their useful comments and corrections. Carrie was particularly helpful in preparing annotations for many of the books listed under "Useful Resources" in each of the chapters and developing sample texts for some of the tasks used in the book.

Chapter 1

The Changing View of Grammar Instruction

Introduction

Grammar is fundamental to language. Without grammar, language does not exist. However, nothing in the field of language pedagogy has been as controversial as the role of grammar teaching. The controversy has always been whether grammar should be taught explicitly through a formal presentation of grammatical rules or implicitly through natural exposure to meaningful language use. According to Kelly (1969), this controversy has existed since the beginning of language teaching. However, whatever position we take regarding grammar instruction, "it is bound to be influenced by the recent history of grammar teaching" (Stern, 1992, p. 140). Therefore, to provide a background to the book, we begin by providing a brief overview of the changes in the teaching of grammar over the years.

Changes in Grammar Teaching

Historically, approaches to grammar teaching have undergone many changes. These changes, which have been due to a number of theoretical and empirical developments in the field, have not been regular and have been characterized by many pendulum swings. They can be viewed in terms of three general instructional approaches, beginning with those that conceptualized teaching in terms of methods with an exclusive focus on grammar, continuing later as types of exposure to meaningful communication, and emerging more recently as a set of instructional options with a focus on both grammar and meaning. In the following sections we will briefly review these changes. We begin by discussing the traditional approaches to grammar instruction, followed by various kinds of communication-based approaches and their limitations and criticisms. We then consider recent developments in grammar pedagogy, including what has come to be known as focus on form (FonF), an instructional option that calls for an integration of grammar and communication in second language (L2) teaching.

Grammar-Based Approaches

For thousands of years, grammar was the center of language pedagogy. Language teaching was equated with grammar teaching and grammar was used as content as well as organizing principles for developing curriculum and language teaching materials (Celce-Murcia, 2001a). It was believed that language was mainly composed of grammar rules and that knowing those rules was sufficient for learners to know the language.

The centrality of grammar in language pedagogy stemmed from various historical reasons. According to Rutherford (1987), one reason had to do with the importance attributed to the knowledge of grammar in philosophy and science in the Middle Ages. During this period, there was also a close relationship between the study of grammar and other medieval disciplines (such as law, theology, and medicine), and the idea that knowledge of grammar was essential for the development of rhetorical skills. It was also believed that the best way of learning an L2 was through studying first language (L1) grammar. This belief led to the idea that the grammar of Latin, which was based on the eight Greek grammatical categories (nouns, verbs, pronouns, prepositions, adverbs, participles, articles, and conjunctions), was the best model for studying other languages (Fotos, 2005). Hence, the formal study of Latin grammar became an important component of the school system. Even when other foreign languages began to be taught in educational settings, the study of Latin grammar was still used as a model for language learning. Studying Latin grammar was also viewed as a means of developing the mind. In the 18th and 19th centuries, other foreign languages were introduced to educational settings (H. D. Brown, 2000). However, it was still believed that the best way of learning the grammar of another language would be through studying the grammar of Latin since it was considered "the model for studying the grammar of any language" (Rutherford 1987, p. 29).

The emphasis on grammar manifested itself in various traditional grammar-based approaches such as the Grammar Translation Method, the Audio-Lingual Method, and other structure-based methods. Although different from one another, these methods are based on the assumption that the major problem in learning a second or foreign language is learning its structure and that this aspect of language must receive exclusive attention.

Grammar Translation and Audio-Lingual Methods

The Grammar Translation Method was introduced towards the end of the 18th century and then spread throughout the world in the 19th century. Different versions of this method are still widely used in many places, particularly in foreign language contexts. Drawing on the approaches used in the teaching of classical languages such as Latin and Greek, this method focused exclusively on studying grammatical rules and structures. Based on categories of Greek and Latin grammar, the target language was segmented into various parts of speech (e.g., nouns, verbs, adverbs, pronouns, articles, participles, conjunctions, and prepositions), which were taught deductively through an explicit explanation of rules, with memorization and translations of texts from the L2 to the L1. With a focus on written language, other purposes of this method included exploring the literature of the target language, preparing learners to develop an understanding of the first language, and training learners' academic capacities.

Towards the end of the 19th and the beginning of the 20th centuries, with the rise of structural linguistics, the focus shifted from studying grammar in terms of parts of speech to a description of its structural and phonological characteristics. With the advent of World War II, a strong need arose for oral communication and the ability to speak foreign languages fluently. These changes, along with developments in behavioral psychology, led to the emergence of the Audio-Lingual and Direct Methods. The Audio-Lingual Method did not present grammatical rules in the same way as the Grammar Translation Method did. However, the focus was still on learning grammatical structures, and not on the development of real-life communication skills. Theoretically, this method was greatly influenced by behaviorist psychology that viewed learning as a process of habit formation and conditioning; thus, it considered memorization of structural patterns essential for L2 learning. It was believed that such memorization formed and reinforced language habits. The Audio-Lingual Method was also influenced by the American school of descriptive and structural linguistics that shifted the focus from studying grammar in terms of parts of speech to a description of its structural and phonological components. As such, lessons in Audio-Lingual teaching consisted mainly of grammatical structures sequenced in a linear manner, usually beginning with an easy structure and ending with more complex forms, with little attention to meaning or context. However, rules were taught inductively through examples and repetition of sentence-level patterns. The emphasis was mainly on developing abilities in oral skills rather than written skills. Instructional units typically began with a conversational dialogue, followed by some pattern drills.

Many other methods emerged after the Grammar Translation and Audio-Lingual methods, such as the Reading Approach, the Oral and Situational Method, the Silent Way, and Total Physical Response. Although they somewhat differed in their underlying assumptions about how language is learned, in terms of syllabus, they were all grammar-based. That is, classroom contents were organized mainly based on analyses of language forms with little focus on language functions or real-life communication. Therefore, they all reflected what Batstone (1994) has characterized as teaching grammar as product, or what Wilkins (1976, p. 2) has characterized as a synthetic approach, in which language is segmented into different parts that are taught one by one in isolation.

Presentation-Practice-Production (PPP) Models

Grammar-based approaches are still used in many L2 classrooms. A very popular form of this approach is the PPP (Presentation-Practice-Production) model of language instruction. According to D. Willis (1996b, p. v), this approach is "so widely accepted that it now forms the basis of many teacher training courses." Different versions of the PPP model can be seen in various language teaching and teacher training textbooks for foreign and second language teachers (e.g., Celce-Murcia & Hilles, 1988; Harmer, 1996; Ur, 1988). The PPP is what many teachers conceive of as a basic lesson structure in many current L2 classrooms (Crookes & Chaudron, 2001).

In the PPP model, grammar instruction consists of a structured three-stage sequence: a presentation stage, a practice stage, and a production stage. In the presentation stage, the new grammar rule or structure is introduced, usually through a text, a dialogue, or a story that includes the structure. The students listen to the text or read it out loud. The main purpose of this stage is to help students become familiar with the new grammatical structure and keep it in their short-term memory (Ur, 1988). The presentation stage is followed by a practice stage, in which students are given various kinds of written and spoken exercises to repeat, manipulate, or reproduce the new forms. The practice stage usually begins with controlled practices that focus learners' attention on specific structures and then moves to less controlled practices with more open-ended activities. The aim of the practice stage is to help students gain control of the knowledge introduced in the presentation stage, to take it in, and to move it from their short-term memory to their long-term memory (Ur, 1988). Finally, in the production stage, learners are encouraged to use the rules they have learned in the presentation and practice stages more freely and in more communicative activities. The aim of this last stage is to fully master the new form by enabling learners to internalize the rules and use them automatically and spontaneously. In a sense, the aim here is to develop fluency.

Theoretically, the PPP model is informed by information processing and skills acquisition models of learning, claiming that language learning is a cognitive skill similar to other kinds of learning. In this view, language is learned by processing information available through input and then accessed for subsequent comprehension and production. Skills acquisition theories (e.g., Anderson, 1982, 1983) claim that learning is a movement from declarative knowledge (i.e., explicit knowledge of rules and systems) to procedural knowledge (i.e., knowledge of how to use the system). Students first learn the new target rules and structures through the development of conscious knowledge, and then practice them in order to gain control of them. In this view, presentation and practice play a key role in the acquisition of language. It is believed that "it is through practice that the material is most thoroughly and permanently learned" (Ur, 1988, p. 10).

Inadequacies of Grammar-Based Approaches

Approaches to grammar instruction that focus on teaching grammar as a set of rules and structures have been found inadequate in meeting the communicative needs of L2 learners. One of the major assumptions underlying traditional grammar-based approaches is that language consists of a series of grammatical forms and structures that can be acquired successively. Grammar teaching is viewed as a deductive and linear presentation of these rules. It is believed that through such presentations of grammar forms, learners are able to develop the kind of knowledge they need for spontaneous language use.

In recent years, however, many researchers have questioned the above assumptions. Reviewing past research on form-focused instruction, Long and Robinson (1998) argued that none of the many studies on L2 learning over the past 30 years shows that presenting grammar rules in a discrete fashion matches the manner in which learners develop language rules. R. Ellis, Basturkmen, and Loewen (2002, p. 421) pointed out:

> While there is substantial evidence that grammar instruction results in learning as measured by discrete-point language tests (e.g., the grammar test in the TOEFL), there is much less evidence to show that it leads to the kind of learning that enables learners to perform the targeted form in free oral production (e.g., in a communicative task).

N. Ellis (2002, p. 175), while not denying the role of explicit instruction, observed that:

> The real stuff of language acquisition is the slow acquisition of form-function mappings and the regularities therein. This skill, like others, takes tens of thousands of hours of practice, practice that cannot be substituted for by provision of a few declarative rules.

Researchers also believe that L2 acquisition is a developmental process and that although there may be individual variations, it follows developmental patterns that are regular and systematic. These sequences, however, are not always amenable to the teachers' teaching agenda. Therefore, learners do not often learn grammatical structures in the order presented by the teacher. Long and Crookes (1992, p. 31) pointed out:

> Where syntax is concerned, research has demonstrated that learners rarely, if ever, move from zero to targetlike mastery of new items in one step. Both naturalistic and classroom learners pass through fixed developmental sequences in word order, negation, questions, relative clauses, and so on—sequences which have to include often quite lengthy stages of nontargetlike use of forms as well as use of nontargetlike forms.

For the same reasons, the underlying assumptions of the more common PPP models have also been questioned. Ellis (2003) argued the PPP models are questionable because they are based on the belief that "practice makes perfect." This notion, he noted, is not appropriate because language acquisition processes appear to be governed by many psychological constraints (Pienemann, 1998). Skehan (1996b) contended that the PPP models are not only inconsistent with the premises of current second language acquisition (SLA) theory, but they are also unsupported by research findings. He pointed out that "the evidence in support of such an approach [PPP] is unimpressive" and that "levels of attainment in conventional language learning are poor, and students commonly leave school with very little in the way of usable language" (p. 18). Skehan (1996b) argued that the reason for the popularity of this method is that is it easy to use, to organize, and to evaluate, and also the teacher is in full control of the structures intended to be covered. Other L2 scholars have criticized the PPP models on the grounds that such models are based on the false assumption that what is taught is, indeed, what is learned (e.g., Scrivener, 1996; D. Willis, 1996a, 1996b). Scrivener (1996) argued that the reason for its popularity is that teachers are trained in this method; hence, they are used to it.

Of course, the PPP model may have its strengths. However, as R. Ellis (2006) pointed out, teaching grammar through presentation and practice of grammatical forms is only one way of teaching grammar. Grammar can also be taught through presentation of rules alone without any practice, or through practice without presentation. It can also be taught through discovering grammatical rules, exposing learners to input that involves occurrences of the target form, or even through corrective feedback provided on learner errors during communicative tasks.

Communication-Based Approaches

The recognition of the inadequacies of approaches that focused exclusively on presentation and manipulation of grammatical forms, and the realization that knowing a language is more than knowing its grammar, led to a shift away from an exclusive focus on language forms to a focus on meaning and language use in communicative contexts. This came to be known as the communicative approach.

The communicative approach defined the aim of language learning as acquiring communicative ability, that is, the ability to use and interpret meaning in real-life communication (Widdowson, 1978), not simply learning formal grammatical rules and structures. This approach was theoretically motivated by various developments in linguistics and sociolinguistics in Europe and North America (Savignon, 2001). A very influential theory was Hymes' theory of "communicative competence" (Hymes, 1972) developed in reaction to Chomsky's (1965) characterization of language competence mainly as linguistic competence. Hymes distinguished between linguistic competence (i.e., knowledge of grammar rules) and communicative competence (i.e., knowledge of language use and the ability to use language), and argued that knowing a language does not simply mean knowing how to produce grammatical sentences accurately but also how to produce them appropriately.

The communicative approach was also influenced by the work of the Council of Europe, which sought to develop syllabi for language learners based on functional use of language, and also the work of other British applied linguists such as Halliday, Firth, Austin, and Searle (e.g., Austin, 1962; Firth, 1957; Halliday, 1978, 1984; Searle, 1969) as well as American sociolinguists such as Gumperz and Labov (e.g., Gumperz & Hymes, 1972; Labov, 1972). These scholars emphasized the importance of studying language use and functions in social contexts.

Other influential factors were developments in SLA theories, particularly Krashen's model of L2 learning and the distinction he made between acquisition and learning (Krashen, 1981, 1985). Krashen defined acquisition as an unconscious and implicit process, and learning as a conscious and explicit one. He argued, and has still argued (Krashen, 2008), that learners should "acquire" language unconsciously and implicitly as a result of exposure to comprehensible input rather than "learn" it consciously through explicit teaching of grammatical rules (Krashen, 1981; Krashen & Terrell, 1983). This view of L2 learning, although not directly associated with communicative language teaching, provided ample theoretical support for its principles and in particular for the role of grammar in language classrooms (Richards & Rodgers, 2001).

Although the communicative approach is generally recognized as an approach that emphasizes meaning-focused language use in language teaching, in terms of methodology, there are no established instructional procedures associated with it, similar to those associated with traditional grammar teaching approaches such as Grammar Translation and Audio-Lingual Methods. Thus, Savignon (2001, p. 27) characterized it as "a theory of ... communicative competence to be used in developing materials and methods appropriate to a given context." Others have taken it to refer to a family of teaching methodologies and syllabi that put the primary focus on developing teaching activities that promote learner abilities in communicating meaning (Nunan, 2004).

However, a number of frameworks have been proposed for implementing the communicative approach in the classroom, which differ from one another in terms of the degree to which they allow a focus on grammatical forms. For example, a distinction has often been made between a weak and a strong version of communicative language teaching (Howatt, 1984). The strong version claims that language is learned through communication; thus, the best way of teaching a language is through activities that are exclusively meaning-focused. In other words, communication is both the goal and the means of language instruction. In the weak version, the end goal is still communication, but learners can learn language in a more controlled manner by using and practicing it in communicative contexts.

The strong version of the communicative approach underlies much of the earlier meaning-focused methods. This includes the notional-functional curriculums (e.g., Brumfit, 1984; DiPietro, 1987; Finocchiaro & Brumfit, 1983), which emphasized language functions as the key organizing principles of language pedagogy, such as greetings, requests, apologies, etc., and also the procedural (Prabhu, 1987), and process-based syllabuses (Breen, 1984; Breen & Candlin, 1980). It also underlies the more recent content-based and immersion models of L2 learning that emphasize integrating language and content, or learning language through subject matter teaching (see Snow, 2001; Snow, Met, & Genesee, 1992). The strong version of the communicative approach has also motivated much of the more recent task-based language instruction. Task-based instruction assumes that central to language learning is engagement in activities that are meaning-focused and are similar in some way to the real-life activities. These activities are called "tasks." There are many definitions of tasks (see Chapter 6), but they all have one thing in common, which is the emphasis on involvement with activities that encourage communicative language use and focus on meaning rather than focus on grammatical forms (Nunan, 2006). Therefore, they all reflect what Batstone (1994, p. 5) termed "teaching as process," where the focus is on "the process of language use," rather than on product, or what Wilkins (1976, p. 13) characterized as an analytic approach, whereby instruction is organized in terms of the purposes for which language is used rather than in terms of its constituent forms.

Although earlier approaches to task-based instruction advocated exclusive attention to meaning (Prabhu, 1984, 1987), later conceptualizations did not rule out the possibility of a focus on linguistic forms. Indeed, most of the recent proposals have emphasized the need for attention to form in L2 task-based teaching (R. Ellis, 2003; Long, 2000; Skehan, 1996a, 1996b, 1998b) (see the next section and also Chapter 6 for a more detailed discussion).

Inadequacies of Communication-Based Approaches

As noted above, although earlier approaches to communicative language teaching advocated exclusive attention to meaning, later conceptualizations did not rule out the possibility of a focus on linguistic forms, with more recent proposals all emphasizing the need for attention to form in L2 task-based teaching. However, the advent of communicative approaches not only weakened the status of grammar teaching, but also led to negative reactions to grammar teaching among many L2 classroom teachers and educators who began to believe that their students' failure was mainly because they had taught them through explicit grammar instruction.

In recent years, however, language-teaching professionals have become increasingly aware that teaching approaches that put the primary focus on meaning with no attention to grammatical forms are inadequate. There is also ample empirical evidence pointing to the shortcomings of such approaches. For instance, extensive studies of French immersion programs have shown that despite ample opportunities of exposure to meaningful content, students do not fully acquire many aspects of the target language available in the input (e.g., Harley & Swain, 1984; Lapkin et al., 1991; Swain, 1985). This research suggests that some type of focus on grammatical forms is necessary if learners are to develop high levels of accuracy in the L2.

In addition, there is strong empirical evidence for the positive effects of instruction that attempts to draw learners' attention to linguistic forms. This evidence comes from a large number of laboratory and classroom-based studies as well as extensive reviews of studies on the effects of form-focused instruction over the past 30 years (e.g., R. Ellis, 1994, 2001b; Larsen-Freeman & Long, 1991; Long, 1983, 1991). In an early review of the literature, Long (1983) concluded that form-focused instruction contributes importantly to language learning. In later reviews, R. Ellis (1994, 2001a, 2001b), N. Ellis (1995), and Larsen-Freeman and Long (1991) found that, while instructed language learning may not have major effects on the sequence of acquisition, it has significant effects on the rate of acquisition and the attainment of accuracy. In a more recent meta-analysis of a large number of studies (49) on the effectiveness of second language instruction, Norris and Ortega (2001) concluded that L2 instruction that focuses on form results in substantial gain in the target structures and that the gains are sustained over time.

Of course, one problem with the studies investigating the role of form-focused instruction is that the measures they used to test learning have favored grammar teaching in the sense that they had measured explicit knowledge through the use of traditional tests such as fill in the blank and sentence transformation exercises (R. Ellis, 2006). Therefore, the evidence has not been definitive. However, the evidence has been strong enough to lead to a re-evaluation of the role of grammar in second language classrooms and the strong conviction that attention to grammatical forms is needed and should not be ignored in language teaching.

Furthermore, although the nature of the link between explicit and implicit knowledge of language has been a matter of debate, a number of SLA researchers have argued that explicit knowledge contributes, if not leads, to acquisition. Some researchers have argued that explicit knowledge may even turn into implicit knowledge if learners are developmentally ready (R. Ellis, 1993b; Pienemann, 1984). It has also been suggested that explicit knowledge can help acquisition in other ways: by producing output that can serve as auto-input to the implicit knowledge system (R. Ellis, 2005), by helping learners monitor their output, and by facilitating the production of unanalyzed language that may contribute to a kind of knowledge that learners may incorporate into their interlanguage system at a later time (Spada & Lightbown, 2008). Lightbown and Spada also argued that when learners are able to produce correct language by using unanalyzed language, they will be able to maintain conversations, which in turn provide them with more comprehensible input. Current research also indicates that learners need ample opportunities to practice and produce structures, which have been taught either explicitly, through a grammar lesson, or taught implicitly, through frequent exposure.

Recent Developments

As mentioned above, there is now ample evidence for the importance of form-focused instruction. However, form-focused instruction refers to grammar instruction that takes place within communicative contexts. It is this perspective on form-focused instruction that has been widely advocated in the literature and has also been supported by SLA research. Reviewing this line of research, Lightbown and Spada (1993, p. 105) concluded:

> [C]lassroom data from a number of studies offer support for the view that form-focused instruction and corrective feedback provided within the context of a communicative program are more effective in promoting second language learning than programs which are limited to an exclusive emphasis on accuracy on the one hand or an exclusive emphasis on fluency on the other.

Focus on Form

In response to the problems presented by traditional approaches to the teaching of grammar, on the one hand, and dissatisfaction with purely communicative approaches on the other, Long (1991) proposed an approach which he termed *focus on form* (FonF). Long distinguished *a focus on form* from *a focus on forms* (FonFs) and *a focus on meaning*. FonFs is the traditional approach. It represents an analytic syllabus, and is based on the assumption that language consists of a series of grammatical forms that can be acquired sequentially and additively. Focus on meaning is synthetic and is based on the assumption that learners are able to analyze language inductively and arrive at its underlying grammar. Thus, it emphasizes pure meaning-based activities with no attention to form. FonF, conversely, is as a kind of instruction that draws the learner's attention to linguistic forms in the context of meaningful communication.

Long claimed that a FonF approach is more effective than both FonFs and focus on meaning and captures "the strength of an analytic approach while dealing with its limitations" (Long & Robinson, 1998, p. 22). Long (2000) argued that FonFs is problematic because it leads to lessons which are dry and consist of teaching linguistic forms with little concern with communicative use. Focus on meaning is problematic because it does not lead to desired levels of grammatical development, is not based on learner needs, and has been found inadequate by studies on meaning-based programs such as French immersion programs (e.g., Harley and Swain 1984; Swain 1985). FonF, on the other hand, meets the conditions most consider optimal for learning. That is, it is learner-centered, represents the learner's internal syllabus, and happens when the learner is attending to meaning and has a communication problem.

Current Views of FonF

The notion of FonF has been widely advocated in the literature. However, since its introduction, this concept has been defined and interpreted differently by different authors. In his conceptualization, Long (1991) characterized FonF mainly as a reaction to linguistic problems that occur during communicative activities. He stated that FonF "overtly draws students' attention to linguistic elements as they arise incidentally in lessons whose overriding focus is on meaning or communication" (Long, 1991, pp. 45–46). He noted that "a syllabus with a focus on form teaches something else—biology, mathematics, workshop practice, automobile repair, the geography of the country where the foreign language is spoken, the cultures of its speakers, and so on" (pp. 45–46). Thus, he excluded drawing learners' attention to form in any predetermined manner. Long believed that learners can acquire most of the grammar of a language incidentally, while their attention is on meaning (Long, 2000). Thus, he assumed that if there is any FonF, it should be brief and occasional.

However, later researchers have expanded the concept of FonF to include both incidental and preplanned, and have also noted that FonF can take place on a broader scale depending on how and when it is administered (e.g., Doughty & Williams, 1998; Lightbown, 1998; Nassaji, 1999; Nassaji & Fotos, 2004, 2007; Spada, 1997; Williams, 2005). Doughty and Williams (1998), for example, suggested that FonF can occur both reactively, by responding to errors, and proactively by addressing possible target language problems before they occur, and that both are reasonable and effective depending on the classroom context. Doughty and Williams also argued that "some focus on form is applicable to the majority of the linguistic code features that learners must master" and that "leaving the learners to their own devices is not the best plan" (1998, p. 197).

R. Ellis (2001b) took a broad perspective on FonF, dividing FonF into planned and incidental. He argued that in both types attention to form occurs while learners' primary focus is on meaning. However, planned FonF differs from incidental FonF in that the former involves drawing learners' attention to pre-selected forms while the latter involves no pre-selection of forms. Also, in incidental FonF, attention to form can occur either reactively, in response to errors during communicative activities, or preemptively, by taking time out from communicative activities to address language forms anticipated to be problematic.

Communicative Approaches Revisited

In keeping with current developments and the recognition of the importance of grammar instruction, in recent years, many of the proposals in language teaching advocate an inclusion of a focus on linguistic forms in classroom instruction. Even the advocates of communicative language teaching have increasingly emphasized the value of attention to form in language learning and classroom pedagogy. For example, in her recent characterization of a communicative approach, Savignon observed that "for the development of communicative ability, research findings overwhelmingly support the integration of form-focused exercises with meaning focused experience." Therefore, she suggested that "the CTL [communicative language teaching] does not exclude a focus on metalinguistic awareness or knowledge of rules of syntax" (Savignon, 2005, p. 645). She pointed out that even traditional activities "such as translation, dictation, and rote memorization can be helpful in bringing attention to form" (Savignon 2001, p. 20).

In keeping with the same trend, many authors have developed frameworks for grammar teaching that emphasize the incorporation of a focus on grammar into meaningful communication (R. Ellis, 1995; R. Ellis & Fotos, 1999; Fotos, 2002; Larsen-Freeman, 2001; Nassaji, 1999). Larsen-Freeman (2001), for example proposed a communicative model of grammar teaching that included three dimensions: form/structure, meaning/semantics, and use/pragmatics. The form/structure dimension refers to the development of knowledge about the formal structure of a language including its syntactic, morphological, and phonological structures. The meaning dimension refers to knowledge about meaning of a language form, and the pragmatic dimension refers to knowledge about when, where and how to use that form. According to Larsen-Freeman, this framework "will be helping ESL/EFL students go a long way toward the goal of being able to accurately convey meaning in the manner they deem appropriate" (2001, p. 255).

Larsen-Freeman (2003) has recently referred to learning grammar skills as *grammaring*, a process whereby the learner becomes able to make use of grammar communicatively (i.e., to use it not only accurately but also meaningfully and appropriately).

Task-based Approaches Revisited

As noted earlier, traditionally, task-based approaches have represented a strong version of the communicative language teaching with no focus on grammar forms. However, current views argue for an inclusion of a grammar focus in task-based instruction (Skehan, 1996b; D. Willis, 1996a, 1996b). For example, in his characterization of task-based instruction, Skehan (1996b, p. 18) suggested when organizing task-based instruction, there needs to be both a focus on language forms and a focus on communication. He argued that "learners do not simply acquire the language to which they are exposed, however carefully that exposure may be orchestrated by the teacher." He argued that in designing task-based instruction, there must be a balance between a focus on grammar forms and a focus on communication. To this end, he outlined three goals for second language task-based pedagogy: *accuracy*, *complexity* and *fluency*. Accuracy was defined as how well language is produced, *complexity* as "the elaboration or ambition of the language which is produced," and *fluency* as the ability to produce language "without undue pausing or hesitation." Skehan (1996b) proposed that effective L2 instruction should strike a balance between these goals because such a balance would not only lead to effective communicative ability but also to "longer-term linguistic development" (p. 18). Of course, the greatest challenge facing teachers is how to find this balance.

D. Willis (1996a) also proposes a task-based model with a heavy focus on form component. His model includes four components: *fluency, accuracy, analysis,* and *conformity. Accuracy* refers to promoting accurate use of language when used for communicative purposes. *Analysis* concerns activities that inform learners of the patterns and regularities in language. *Conformity* refers to activities that are teacher controlled and are used to promote consciousness-raising such as those related to controlled repetitions of fixed phrases, various types of form-focused activities, and the provision of form-focused summaries of what learners have learned at the end of each lesson. Finally, J. Willis (1996) has proposed a task-based framework very similar to the grammar-based PPP model, with the difference that the order of the meaning-based and form-based activities is reversed. Her model consists of three cycles: pre-task cycle, task cycle, and language focus cycle. The aim of the pre-task phase is to expose students to the task or prepare them to carry out the task, through such activities as brainstorming, using pictures, highlighting new vocabulary, etc. The task cycle is to give them opportunities to use the language for spontaneous communication. The language focus phase is to help them develop an awareness of how language works, which can be achieved through the use of various language-based activities and exercises such as repetition, sentence completion, matching exercises, dictionary work, etc.

The above task-based frameworks may be different from one another in certain ways. But what they all share is an emphasis on grammar and an attempt to find a proper place for a FonF in L2 pedagogy (see Chapter 6).

Our Conception of FonF

In this book, we conceive of FonF in broad terms. Since our motivation is driven by pedagogical considerations, we conceive of FonF as a series of methodological options that, while adhering to the principles of communicative language teaching, attempt to maintain a focus on linguistic forms in various ways. Such a focus can be attained explicitly and implicitly, deductively or inductively, with or without prior planning, and integratively or sequentially. We also believe that FonF must be a component of a broader L2 instructed learning that should provide ample opportunities for meaningful and form-focused instruction and also a range of opportunities for L2 input, output, interaction, and practice (see Fotos & Nassaji, 2007). Following R. Ellis (2001b) and Williams (2005), we also adopt a broad definition of the term "form," taking it to include various formal components of language including grammatical, phonological, lexical, and pragmatic forms. In short, we believe that FonF must be a component of a broader L2 instructed learning that provides ample opportunities for meaningful and form-focused instruction including a range of opportunities for L2 input, output, interaction, and practice. It should be approached in ways that are responsive to the needs of the learners, takes into account the various context-related variables, and considers learner characteristics including, their age, developmental readiness, and other individual differences (see Chapter 8). The sequential option takes place when the teaching of grammar occurs in separate mini lessons followed or preceded by communicative activities. This approach is especially important for the foreign language situation where target language access is limited.

Conclusion

In this chapter, we provided a brief overview of the changes in teaching grammar over the years. We also examined current developments in grammar teaching and communicative FonF. As noted, in recent years, teachers, teacher educators, and researchers seem to largely agree on the importance of grammar instruction, and consequently have attempted to develop frameworks and proposals to promote a focus on grammar in L2 communicative classrooms. Indeed, if the goal of second language learning is to develop communicative competence and to enable learners to use language accurately and fluently for real communicative purposes, a focus on grammar must be incorporated into L2 communicative instruction. In the following chapters, we will explore a number of proposals that current SLA research suggests regarding how a focus on grammar can be integrated with a focus on communication in L2 teaching. R. Ellis (2006) pointed out that we need to know whether and to what extent proposals for teaching grammar are compatible with how learners learn grammar. Therefore, we not only describe each of the options proposed but also explore their theoretical underpinnings, and see to what extent they are supported by current research.

Questions for Reflection

1 What do you think have been the major influential factors that have led to the changes in views of teaching grammar over the years? Do you see any value in traditional grammar-based approaches such as the Grammar Translation Method or the Audio-Lingual Method? What is the evidence for the claim that grammar instruction within a communicative context contributes to the development of second language competence?
2 How significant is it to distinguish between a weak and a strong version of communicative language teaching? Do you think this distinction is necessary? If so, where does the PPP approach that combines grammar exercises with free communicative activities fit into this distinction? Do you feel that the criticisms leveled at the PPP approaches are justified?

3   How does the role of grammar teaching differ in its significance for children and adults? What are the factors that you think would distinguish these two groups of learners?

4   Do you think that a FonF approach is more effective than a FonFs approach? Why? Do you think that a FonF approach is suitable for all learners at all levels of language proficiency? Do you think any adjustments should be made to this approach to make it suitable for your own teaching situation?

5   How do you distinguish between task-based instruction and communicative language teaching? In what ways are they similar? It what way are they different? Some may argue that a task-based approach suffers from the same problem of narrowness of approach that a grammatical approach suffers from, except with an emphasis on meaning at the expense of form, as opposed to form at the expense of meaning. What do you think?

Useful Resources

Batstone, R. (1994). *Grammar*. Oxford: Oxford University Press.
This handbook is a useful guide for implementing grammar instruction and applying it to communicative practices. Targeted primarily for teachers, this book puts together a framework by which teachers can implement these approaches on an integrated level, as each section is interrelated, which allows for strategy development within pedagogy.

Celce-Murcia, M. (2001). "Language teaching approaches: An overview." In M. Celce-Murcia (Ed.), *Teaching English as a second or foreign language* (pp. 3–11). Boston: Heinle & Heinle.
This chapter looks at the history of language teaching and suggests that awareness of the history of specific methodologies can influence the approaches used in language teaching. It gives a survey of the many trends in language teaching, beginning with methodologies existing prior to the 20th century, and follows through with nine of the most common approaches to language teaching in the past hundred years. This is useful for language instructors because it gives the most significant features of each approach, and accounts for both the strengths and weaknesses of each methodology.

Doughty, C. & Williams, J. (Eds.). (1998). *Focus on form in classroom language acquisition*. Cambridge: Cambridge University Press.
This volume is a compilation of papers that summarize research and theory of the focus on form method. It gives a comprehensive discussion of a variety of issues related to focus on form and its implementation in L2 classrooms. This book also gives the reader an insight into the nature of the controversy surrounding form-focused instruction and its implications within an ever-shifting pedagogical pendulum.

Fotos, S., & Nassaji, H. (Eds.). (2007). *Form focused instruction and teacher education: Studies in honour of Rod Ellis*. Oxford: Oxford University Press.

This volume provides a useful discussion of a wide range of current topics concerning form-focused instruction and teacher education. It examines both theoretical and empirical issues and also considers how focus on form can be effectively integrated into communicative pedagogy. This is a useful resource for teachers, teacher educators, and researchers interested in the role of form-focused instruction in L2 teacher education.

Richards, J. C., & Rodgers, T. (1986). *Approaches and methods in language teaching: A description and analysis.* Cambridge: Cambridge University Press. This handbook gives an account of some of the most common methods of second language teaching in the 20th century. The book seeks to give an objective account of these approaches in order to give teachers an in-depth look at the strengths and weaknesses of various frameworks, allowing readers to come to their own conclusions about what a teaching framework should look like. These features make this book useful for teachers and teacher trainees alike.

Part I

Input-based Options in Focus on Grammar

Chapter 2

Focus on Grammar through Processing Instruction

Introduction

In this chapter, we will discuss how grammar can be focused on in L2 classrooms through processing instruction. Processing instruction is a particular approach to teaching grammar that is based on how learners interpret and process input for meaning. This approach rests on the assumption that the role of input is central to language acquisition and that grammar can best be learned when learners attend to it in input-rich environments. Theoretically, the approach draws on a model of input processing developed by VanPatten and his colleagues (Lee & VanPatten, 2003; VanPatten, 1996, 2002a). In this approach, an initial exposure to explicit instruction is combined with a series of input-processing activities that aim to help learners create form-meaning connections as they process grammar for meaning. Due to the explicit grammar component of processing instruction, some researchers have equated it with a focus on forms approach (e.g., R. Sheen, 2007). However, VanPatten (2002a) has argued that since the aim of this approach is "to assist the learner in making form–meaning connections during IP [input processing]; it is more appropriate to view it as a type of focus on form" (p. 764) (see Chapter 1 for the distinction between focus on form and focus on forms).

We will begin by briefly reviewing the importance of input in L2 acquisition, and then discuss the theoretical background of processing instruction, which is VanPatten's input processing model. We will then describe processing instruction as a pedagogical technique that rests on the principles of the input-processing model (please note the difference between processing instruction as a pedagogical technique and input processing as a theoretical model). Next, we will review the empirical research that has examined the effectiveness of processing instruction. Finally, we will provide examples of classroom activities based on input processing principles.

Input and its Role in Language Learning

Although there have been different perspectives on the nature of input and its contribution to language learning, the importance of its role in language acquisition cannot be disputed. Gass (1997) described input as "the single most important concept of second language acquisition" (p. 1). Input can be defined as the language "that learners hear or see to which they attend for its propositional content (message)" (VanPatten, 1996, p. 10). In other words, it is the sample of language that the learners are exposed to and attempt to process for meaning. Input can be both oral and written. For example, when someone is listening to the radio or watching TV, he or she is exposed to oral input. When the person is reading or browsing a newspaper, he is exposed to written input.

As discussed by R. Ellis (1999), the centrality of the role of input in language acquisition has been emphasized by a number of SLA theories. One such theory is Universal Grammar (UG), which posits that human beings are biologically endowed with an innate ability to learn language. Such an ability is assumed to explain how child L1 learners are capable of developing such a complex system of language in such a short period of time (see also Chapter 8). To explain this ability, it is assumed that there is an innate language-specific module in the mind that contains a set of general and abstract language-specific principles and parameters, and that it is this module that determines what specific shape a language should take. In the UG approach, the role of input is essential because input drives language acquisition by triggering the UG mechanisms, enabling learners to set the UG parameters according to the different kinds of input in the environment.

Another theory that emphasizes the importance of input is the information-processing perspective (e.g., McLaughlin, 1990; McLeod & McLaughlin, 1986; Shiffrin & Schneider, 1977). This theory holds that learning a language is like other kinds of learning, and is driven by general cognitive processes. This perspective distinguishes between two cognitive stages of language acquisition: controlled and automatic. Controlled processes are not yet learned processes and remain under the attentional control of the learner. Thus, they usually require a large amount of processing capacity and more time for activation. Automatic processes are fast and demand relatively little processing capacity. In information processing theories, the role of input is crucial because it is the information in the input and its frequency that help learners form a mental representation of the target language.

Another theoretical perspective that underscores the role of input is skill-acquisition theories. Similar to information processing theories, skill-acquisition theories also conceptualize language learning as a complex skill that involves several cognitive stages (e.g., Anderson, 1982, 1983). In this view, a distinction is made between declarative and procedural knowledge. Declarative knowledge is knowledge about language, and procedural knowledge is knowledge of how to use it. In this view, all knowledge is initially declarative, and then becomes procedural through ample practice. In skill-acquisition theories, input is essential because it forms learners' initial declarative knowledge.

All the above theories emphasize the centrality of input. Although their perspectives on its exact role are different, each highlights the importance of input in assisting language acquisition.

Input Processing

VanPatten has defined input processing as strategies that learners use to link grammatical forms to their meanings or functions. In other words, input processing "attempts to explain how learners get form from input and how they parse sentences during the act of comprehension while their primary attention is on meaning" (VanPatten, 2002a, p. 757). A key concept here is the term "processing." In his discussion, VanPatten has made a distinction between processing and other related concepts, such as perception, noticing, and intake. Whereas *processing* refers to the mechanism used in drawing meaning from input, *perception* refers to the registration of acoustic signals present in an utterance that the learner hears. *Noticing* refers to the conscious registration of those forms in memory. Both perception and noticing can take place prior to or without assigning any meaning to a particular form. However, processing involves both perception and noticing and also assigning meaning to the form. *Intake* refers to that part of the input that the learner has noticed and has stored in his or her working memory for further processing. Thus, intake is what becomes the basis of language learning. It is the intake that becomes internalized and incorporated in the learner's language. Based on the limited capacity model of human cognition, VanPatten (1996) has argued that one problem L2 learners have in processing input is the difficulty in attending to form and meaning at the same time. He proposes that learners may either focus on meaning only without paying adequate attention to form or may focus on form without adequately processing meaning. To deal with this problem, he has argued, learners should be taught how to process input correctly so that they can learn the underlying grammar while their attention is on meaning. To this end, he maintained, we first need to know how learners process input, and then design instruction in such a way that helps learners create the kind of form-meaning connection needed for learning. Thus, the rationale behind processing instruction can be summarized as follows:

1 Learners need input for acquisition.
2 A major problem in acquisition might be the way in which learners process input.
3 If we can understand how learners process input, then we might be able to devise effective input enhancement or focus on form to aid acquisition of formal features of language (VanPatten, 2009, p. 48).

VanPatten's Input Processing Model

In his work, VanPatten has outlined an input processing model that has tried to show how learners process input in their memory and how they derive intake from input while their focus is on meaning. Central to this theory are the following questions: (1) How does the learner process the input to which he or she is exposed?; (2) What is it that makes some input more difficult to process than other input?; and (3) What are the processes that impede or delay the acquisition of input? VanPatten has warned that his model is not a model of L2 acquisition because input processing is only one of the processes that are involved in SLA. SLA is complex and involves many processes and sub-processes that work together. It is also not a complete model of how L2 learners parse L2 sentences or how this process might work. But it is an attempt to describe the initial processes that learners use when acquiring an L2. In addition, a focus on input does not suggest that output is not essential as both are needed for acquisition. But the input processing model rests on the assumption that the primary source of data for language acquisition is input. VanPatten's model contains the following four main principles:

1   Learners process input for meaning before they process it for form.
2   For learners to process form that is not meaningful, they must be able to process informational or communicative content at no or little cost to attention.
3   Learners possess a default strategy that assigns the role of agent (or subject) to the first noun (phrase) they encounter in a sentence/utterance. This is called the first noun strategy.
4   Learners first process elements in sentence/utterance initial position.

Principle 1 (also called the primacy of meaning principle) suggests that when processing input, learners first look for meaning in the input. This priority along with the limitations of the working memory capacity prevents some parts of the form in the input from being processed for acquisition. The working memory constraints also affect comprehension as learners first pay attention to those words that carry the most meaning, which are mostly the content words. Because of the efforts to process content words, other smaller words (such as function words or inflections) may not be processed. If they are, they may be partially processed in the working memory. In addition, language forms are not equal in the degree of meaning they express (that is, some may carry less information than others). Thus, learners may tend to pay more attention to forms that express more meaning than those that express less meaning. According to VanPatten, natural languages are characteristically redundant. That is, the same information is encoded more than once, such as in a sentence that contains a third person subject and a third person singular-s. Both of these forms (i.e., the subject and the grammatical singular-s) carry the same semantic meaning. However when processing input, the learner might tend to focus on the main lexical item to get that information. Therefore he or she may not notice the inflection, and if he or she notices it, it may not be processed adequately.

Principle 2 concerns processing forms that do not express meaning or do not contribute much to the overall meaning of the utterance. As noted earlier, learners' memory resources constrain what learners can attend to during comprehension. Consequently learners may tend not to use their attentional resources for processing items that may not have much communicative value or do not contribute much to meaning. Thus, Principle 2 states that in order for learners to process forms that have little communicative values, they must be able to process the overall communicative content at little or no cost to attention. In other words, forms that do not have much communicative value will be attended to only when attentional resources required for processing meaning have not been used up. A corollary of this principle is that those items are usually learned later in acquisition. According to VanPatten, there is no direct empirical support for this principle but there is some indirect evidence that this might be the case. One piece of evidence, for example, would be the order in which learners of English acquire the verb morpheme -ing followed by the regular past, followed by the third person -s. The reason for this, VanPatten argues, could be that -ing has a higher communicative value than the third person singular -s.

Principle 3 concerns the order of words in a sentence and how learners process them. According to this principle, to derive meaning from a sentence, learners should assign roles to the different words in a sentence. That is, they need to know who has done what. According to Principle 3, learners usually assign the role of agent to "the first noun" in the sentence when processing input. According to VanPatten (1996), this first-noun strategy works successfully in languages where the subject of the sentence is usually the first word, such as in English with its subject–verb–object (SVO) word order, but not in languages that do not have such a word order or may have a more flexible word order, like Spanish.

Principle 4 suggests that the salience of grammatical forms may differ depending on where they occur in the sentence. According to this principle, the initial word in a sentence is more salient than the medial or final word. Therefore, learners pay more attention to the words that are in an initial position in a sentence. Thus, they process and learn these words more quickly than those which appear in other positions. According to VanPatten (2002a), this may explain why learners may not need to be instructed that Spanish has subject–verb inversion in yes/no questions because they can immediately notice the inversion in the input. However, they have a harder time understanding how object pronouns work because they do not encounter them in the initial position.

Processing Instruction

Processing instruction is a pedagogical technique that is based on the principles of the input processing model described above. This kind of instruction rests on the assumption that by understanding how learners process input, we will be able to devise effective instructional activities to aid input processing for acquisition and, at the same time, learn the forms that are contained in the input. The key components of processing instruction as a pedagogical intervention are as follows:

1   Learners are provided with information about the target linguistic form or structure.
2   They are informed of the input processing strategies that may negatively affect their processing of the target structure.
3   They carry out input-based activities that help them understand and process the form during comprehension.

As noted earlier, one of the principles of the input processing model is that when learners are confronted with input, they first pay attention to content over form. This strategy can have negative effects on learning redundant forms because students may not attend to those target forms. Processing instruction aims to help learners to process such input correctly and to create the kind of form–meaning connection needed for learning. To see how these characteristics work in practice, take the following example:

Suppose that the teacher has noticed students have difficulty supplying the plural -s when using it in their utterance in English. According to the input processing model, learners may not process this linguistic feature when they hear it in a sentence such as "He has two cars" because of the redundancy of the information in the input. In other words, learners may successfully comprehend the meaning of the sentence without the need to attend to the plural-s. The teacher can address this problem by using the processing instruction technique. To this end the teacher can first begin by giving students some explicit information about how plural forms are structured in English (component #1). The aim of this explanation is not to teach the learners grammar but to direct their attention to the problem. After this brief explanation, the teacher may inform the learners of why they tend to ignore the plural-s when they normally read or listen to input that contains that form (component #2). Finally, the teacher would use a number of input-based activities that are specifically designed to help learners to process the plural-s correctly for meaning (component #3). For example, he or she may use sentence-matching tasks in which students read or listen to a series of sentences and decide whether the sentences match with a set of drawings. To do this task, learners must pay attention to the content. In addition, in order to be able to decide correctly, they have to pay attention to the plural-s. The teacher may also use listening tasks in which students have to listen to a set of sentences and recognize the correct meaning.

Empirical Evidence for Processing Instruction

A number of studies have examined the role of processing instruction in learning grammatical forms. These studies have been mainly conducted in classroom contexts and have compared processing instruction with the more traditional grammar instruction that involves presentation of grammar rules and structures followed by production practices. The studies are motivated by the hypothesis that processing instruction may have superior effects over traditional grammar instruction because the former provides learners with opportunities to convert input to intake. According to VanPatten (2004), processing instruction targets language acquisition at the initial stage of processing, which is input processing. This instruction not only affects learners' input processing strategies but also affects their underlying system in such a way that they will eventually be able to incorporate the target form in their output. The difference between the traditional grammar instruction and processing instruction has been illustrated in Cadierno (1995) as shown in Figures 2.1 and 2.2.

As illustrated, both models contain the three main processes considered essential for language acquisition, namely input, intake, and output. However, the difference is where the instruction occurs.

The first series of studies that compared the effectiveness of processing instruction (Figure 2.1) with that of traditional grammar instruction (Figure 2.2) were conducted by VanPatten and his co-researchers on learning L2 Spanish morphology (Cadierno, 1995; VanPatten & Cadierno, 1993). Later research examined this approach in other languages and on learning other target structures.

One of the earliest studies was by VanPatten and Cadierno (1993), who compared the effectiveness of processing instruction in the acquisition of Spanish clitic object pronouns. This target structure was used based on the assumption that learners of Spanish have difficulty processing these forms.

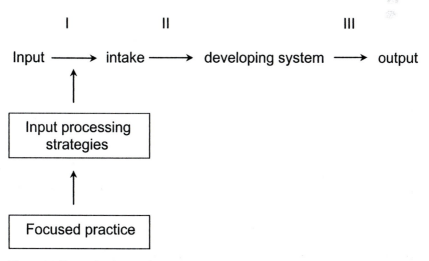

Figure 2.1 Processing instruction

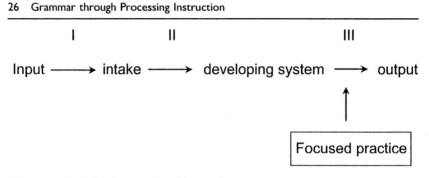

Figure 2.2 Traditional output-based instruction

Three groups of learners participated in the study: (1) a group that received traditional instruction (explicit instruction plus output practice); (2) a group that received processing instruction (information about how to interpret the input correctly plus structured input activities); and (3) a third group that was the control group, receiving no instruction. The study found that learners who received processing instruction outperformed those who received output-based instruction on both comprehension and production tests. Cadierno (1995) conducted a similar study using Spanish past tense verb morphology and found results similar to those of VanPatten and Cadierno (1993). That is, the processing instruction group outperformed the other groups on interpretation tasks and performed similar to the output group on the production task.

VanPatten and Oikkenon (1996) conducted a study to find out which of the two components of processing instruction (explicit instruction and structured input) are responsible for creating the advantageous effects in previous studies. The target structure was object pronoun placement in Spanish. Three experimental groups participated in the study, a group receiving grammatical information along with input processing activities, a group receiving grammatical explanation only, and a third group receiving processing instruction only. Their results showed the advantage of processing instruction was due to input processing activities not explicit instruction (see Benati, 2001, 2004 for similar results).

A number of other studies have also investigated the beneficial effects of processing instruction (e.g., Allen, 2000; Benati, 2001, 2004; Cheng, 2002; Erlam, 2003; Farley, 2001; Morgan-Short & Bowden, 2006; Toth, 2006). These studies have yielded important but different results. While some have shown that both input- and output-based instruction are equally effective in helping learners learn target structures (e.g., Cheng, 2002; Farley, 2001), others have shown that the effects of instruction also depend on other factors, such as the target grammatical form, type of tasks or language measures used (e.g., Allen, 2000; Benati, 2001). Farley (2001), for example, compared the effects of processing instruction with meaning-based output instruction on the acquisition of the Spanish subjunctive. Two groups of learners participated in the study each receiving one of the treatments. The results of interpretation and output tasks showed no significant differences between the two groups in production tasks. However, processing instruction has greater effects on learners' ability to interpret the target forms. Therefore, the results of Farley were different from those studies that had shown an advantage for processing instruction on both interpreting and producing the target structures. Farley explained that part of the reason could be that the output tasks used in the study involved meaning-focused activities that also involved input.

Cheng (2002) compared the effects of input processing instruction and traditional instruction on the acquisition of the Spanish copula verbs *ser* and *estar*. Three groups of learners participated in the study: (1) a group that received traditional instruction (explicit grammar instruction along with production practices); (2) a group that received processing instruction; and (3) a control group that received no instruction. To assess the effects of treatments, three kinds of tasks were used: an oral interpretation task, a sentence production task, and a guided composition task. The results showed that the groups that received processing instruction and traditional instruction outperformed the control group on all three measurement tasks, but there was no significant difference between the traditional instruction group on any of the post-tests. Thus, these results also differ from those reported by VanPatten and Cadierno (1993), which showed superior effects for processing instruction, when compared to traditional instruction in enabling learners to interpret the target structure.

Some studies have also shown that while input-based instruction may be more effective for improving comprehension skills, output-based instruction may be more effective for improving production skills (see DeKeyser, Salaberry, Robinson, & Harrington, 2002, for a review). A few studies have also shown benefits for output-based instruction different from those for input-based instruction. For example, Toth (2006) showed that learners who were engaged in producing output outperformed the groups who received processing instruction. Output also promoted mental processes (such as meta-linguistic analysis of language forms), which were different from the processes involved in input processing. Erlam (2003), using measures of both listening comprehension and written production, found greater effects for output-based instruction than input-based instruction.

The conclusion that one can draw from this research is that when used in combination with explicit instruction, processing instruction may be helpful, particularly in enhancing learners' abilities to comprehend the target form. In other words, processing instruction may be more effective for promoting comprehension skills whereas production-based instruction may be more effective for promoting production skills. In addition, the effectiveness of processing instruction may depend on a number of variables, including the type of linguistic feature the learner is supposed to learn, the length of the testing time, and the learners' level of language proficiency.

Structured Input

Classroom activities that are used in input-processing instruction are called structured input. They are so called because they are specifically designed to contain input that facilitates form-meaning connections. They are designed to force students to focus on the target structure and to process it for meaning. They are also designed to discourage learners from using processing strategies that negatively affect comprehension. According to VanPatten (2004), input processing strategies are context neutral, that is, they are not affected by classroom or non-classroom contexts and are used in all circumstances. Therefore, structured input activities are useful for both ESL and EFL contexts.

Structured input activities are of two main types: referential and affective (VanPatten, 1996). Referential activities are activities for which there is always a right or wrong answer. For example, learners can be asked to choose between two noun phrases that have been associated with a drawing (e.g., a singular and a plural). In these activities there is a right or wrong answer, and the learners' right answers reveal that that they have understood the meaning correctly. Affective activities are those that do not have any right or wrong answer. These activities require learners to provide an affective response by indicating their agreements or opinions about a set of events. For example, these could involve tasks that require learners to respond to what they have heard or read by checking boxes labeled "agree" or "disagree" (see the following section for examples). Structured input activities can involve both oral and written activities. For example, the teacher may use reading activities in which students read a series of sentences and attempt to respond to them or listening activities in which learners listen to a set of sentences and try to process the correct meaning.

Guidelines for Developing Structured Input Activities

Lee and VanPatten (2003) and VanPatten (1993) have suggested a number of guidelines for developing structured input activities. These guidelines have been discussed in other places such as in Farley (2005) and Wong (2005). These researchers have all emphasized that these guidelines are important and should be considered in designing effective input processing materials. Thus, we will briefly present them here.

Keep Meaning in Focus

The aim of input processing activities is to enhance form-meaning connections. This guideline also highlights the importance of communicative meaning-based activities and the idea that acquisition cannot take place successfully through meaningless rote learning.

Present One Item at a Time

In structured input activities items should be presented one a time. This ensures that there is no need for too much explicit explanation, which will otherwise make the lesson a complete grammar lesson. This also ensures that learners' attentional resources are not drained by attempting to process too much information. By presenting one item at a time, the teacher also has time to use other related communicative structured input activities about those forms.

Use Oral and Written Input

Structured input activities should use both written and oral input. Both modes of presentation should be used to ensure that learners' individual differences have been addressed (VanPatten, 1993). For example, some learners may be visual learners. That is, they may learn better when they see something and benefit more from visual input such as that found with reading activities. Others may be more auditory-oriented; therefore, they may benefit more from the auditory input presented with listening activities.

Move from Individual Sentences to Connected Discourse

Good input processing activities are those that begin with short utterances and move gradually to larger pieces of discourse. The reason for this is that short sentences are easier to process, particularly at beginner levels. Thus, it is easier for learners to pay attention to the target form. However, since learners should eventually process input at the discourse level, it would be advisable to gradually expose them to connected discourse.

Have Learners Do Something with the Input

When learners are presented with input, they should not simply listen to or read the input. Rather, they should be required to take some action in response to it to ensure that the learner is processing the input for meaning. There are different ways of doing so. For instance, learners may be presented with a set of statements and asked to decide whether they are true of false, or whether they agree or disagree with them. They may also be asked to match statements, words, or phrases with pictures.

Keep Learners' Processing Strategies in Mind

The aim of input-processing instruction is to help learners overcome their faulty input processing strategies. Therefore, when designing structured input activities, the teacher should have those processing strategies in mind so that he or she can design appropriate activities that can assist learners to process the input correctly. As Wong (2005) noted, the fact that learners are exposed to an activity that involves input does not indicate that the activity is a structured input activity. For a task to be so, it should be able to push the learner to bypass an unhelpful processing strategy and then attend to the form while processing the input for meaning. This suggests that the teacher should first know what the problematic input processing strategy is and what it is that hinders the learner to process the form correctly. Once these strategies are identified, then the teacher can begin designing the structured input activities. For example, "If learners are relying on lexical items to interpret tense (Principle 1), then we may want to structure the activities so that learners are pushed to rely on grammatical morphemes instead of lexical adverbs to get tense" (Wong, 2005, p. 42).

Classroom Activities: Examples of Structured Input Activities

In this section, we will present examples of structured input activities that can be used to provide learners with opportunities to focus on grammar while processing input. These examples are modeled after published work in this area, including the works of VanPatten and his colleagues. We provide examples of both referential and affective activities. As noted earlier, referential activities are those that involve only one correct answer. Affective activities do not have any right or wrong answer; learners have to simply indicate their agreement or opinions about a set of sentences. Classroom teachers can use these activities separately or in combination.

Referential Activities

The following three activities provide examples of referential activities. Recall that referential activities are activities for which there is always a right or wrong answer. They can be used for students in upper-beginner or lower-intermediate level classes. The aim of the first two activities is to help learners with the acquisition of English past and future tenses, respectively. The third activity facilitates learning causative constructions.

According to the input-processing model, learners prefer processing lexical items to morphological items. Since tenses in English can be marked both morphologically and lexically, learners may not process the morphological marker if the tense is also marked lexically with a time reference, such as an adverb of time. The goal of activity 1 is to push learners to process the morphological marker -ed, which they may not otherwise notice if the past adverbial is provided.

Activity 1

Instruction: Listen to the following sentences and decide whether they describe an action that was done before or is usually done.

	Now	*Before*
1. The teacher corrected the essays.	☐	☐
2. The man cleaned the table.	☐	☐
3. I wake up at 5 in the morning.	☐	☐
4. The train leaves the station at 8 am.	☐	☐
5. The writer finished writing the book.	☐	☐
6. The trees go green in the spring.	☐	☐

Activity 2

Activity 2 focuses on the English future tense. In this activity, the time referent has been omitted from the statements. Therefore, to process the tense of the sentence, the learner must pay attention to the morphological marker. Similar activities can be designed with a focus on other tenses.

Instruction: Read the following statements and decide whether the person is talking about what he currently does or what he will do when he retires.

	Now	*Retirement*
1. I meet new people.	☐	☐
2. I will travel a lot.	☐	☐
3. I will work hard.	☐	☐
4. I give money to charities.	☐	☐
5. I will be happy.	☐	☐
6. I am a role model.	☐	☐
7. I play soccer.	☐	☐
8. I will hold many parties.	☐	☐

Activity 3

One of the grammatical forms that may be difficult for English language learners is causative construction, sentences in which someone is caused to do something. Examples of such constructions include: "I had my students write an essay" and "I made the man clean the room." Since these sentences include two agents, according to the input processing model, students may always assign the role of the person who did the activity to the first noun. Therefore, they may have problems interpreting the statements accurately. For example, in the sentence "John had his student write an essay," students may incorrectly interpret it as "John wrote the essay." A structured input activity such as the following can be designed to help learners to interpret such statements accurately.

Students' instruction: Listen to each of the following sentences and then decide who is performing the action by checking the box.

The teacher's instructions: Read each sentence only once and then, after each sentence, ask for an answer. Do not wait until the end to review answers. Students do not repeat or otherwise produce the structure.

1 The girl made the man check the house for mice.
2 My dad made my brother babysit the children all night.
3 Mom let the boys go to three different circuses in one week.
4 The boss had the chef prepare several roast geese for the wedding dinner.
5 Jack let Joe collect some of the data required for our project.
6 The professor had the students create hypotheses for their science experiment.

1. Who checked the house for mice?	The girl	☐	The man	☐
2. Who babysat the children all night?	My dad	☐	My brother	☐
3. Who went to three different circuses in one week?	Mom	☐	The boys	☐
4. Who prepared several roast geese for the wedding dinner?	The boss	☐	The chef	☐
5. Who collected some of the data required for our project?	Jack	☐	Joe	☐
6. Who had the students create hypotheses for their science experiment?	The professor	☐	The students	☐

Affective Activities

The following two activities provide examples of affective activities. Recall that affective activities require learners to express their opinion and do not have right or wrong answers. They can be used with students in a lower-intermediate level class. The aim of the first activity is to push students to process the present and past participle adjectives. The aim of the second activity is to help learners process the simple past tense. The activities can be conducted orally or in written forms.

Activity 4

Instruction: Read the following sentences and decide whether you agree with the statement.

	Agree	Disagree
1. The book was boring.	☐	☐
2. I am bored when someone tells a joke.	☐	☐
3. People who gossip a lot are very irritating.	☐	☐
4. I get irritated with small talk.	☐	☐
5. It is interesting to talk about yourself.	☐	☐
6. The book was interesting.	☐	☐

Activity 5

Step 1: Read the following activities and indicate whether you did the same things over the weekend.

	Yes	No
1. I did my homework.	☐	☐
2. I watched TV.	☐	☐
3. I wrote a letter to my friend.	☐	☐
4. I had a birthday party.	☐	☐
5. I walked to the beach.	☐	☐
6. I cleaned my room.	☐	☐
7. I went downtown.	☐	☐
8. I rode my bike.	☐	☐

Step 2: Now form pairs and compare your responses with your classmate to see whether he or she did the same activities.

Conclusion

In this chapter, we discussed processing instruction as an option in teaching grammar communicatively in L2 classrooms. This option can be a useful technique in helping learners to attend to form in the context of understanding message content. However, like any other instructional strategy, it has its own shortcomings and limitations. One of the limitations, for example, is that processing instruction can address only certain linguistic forms or constructions that have transparent form-meaning relationships. For example, it would be difficult to see how input processing tasks can be designed so that they can help learners to correctly process articles in English. Such forms have complex form–meaning relationships and also their understanding always depends on the context in which the form is used. Another limitation is that it does not require learners to produce output. This, of course, does not mean output is not essential or less important than input. VanPatten (e.g., VanPatten, 1993, 2002a) has warned that although processing instruction emphasizes the role of input, this does not negate the importance of output. Production may play a crucial role in the development of fluency, accuracy and automatization of various aspects of language. This suggests that to be fully effective, teaching grammar should involve learners with ample opportunities for both input and output. Therefore, we recommend that teachers should view processing instruction as only one of the options in their tool kit for teaching grammar. To increase its effectiveness, teachers should combine structured input activities with other classroom activities, including output and interactive tasks and corrective feedback on learner errors. Teachers should also feel free to adapt or make any changes they deem necessary to structured input activities based on the contexts of their teaching and their learners' goals and objectives. This would ensure that the activities used are maximally effective.

Questions for Reflection

1 Do you think that processing instruction can also be used for teaching other language skills such as pronunciation or vocabulary? If so, consider a situation in which you want to teach an aspect of pronunciation. How would you design a structured input activity that can be used to teach that aspect of the target language?
2 As we have discussed in this chapter, processing instruction supporters believe that the difficulty of processing input is mainly due to inappropriate processing strategies learners use. Do you think that other linguistic, psychological, social factors or even learners' attitudes towards learning the language may also play a role? If so, why?
3 List a few grammar features that you think can be taught through processing instruction. Design structured input activities that can be used to teach them. List a few features that you think cannot be taught through processing instruction. What kind of grammar-focused activities would you use to teach them?
4 How do you distinguish between structured input activities and other listening or reading activities that teachers use in their classrooms? What are the differences and similarities?

Useful Resources

Benati, A., & Lee, J. (2008). *Grammar acquisition and processing instruction: Secondary and cumulative effects.* Clevedon: Multilingual Matters.
This book provides a useful introduction to processing instruction and examines its secondary and cumulative effects. Secondary effects refer to the effects of processing instruction on structures that are similar to those targeted by the instruction, and cumulative effects are those that carry over to different target structures. The book also includes a useful appendix that provides the input processing materials used in other studies.

Farley, A. P. (2005). *Structured input: Grammar instruction for the acquisition-oriented classroom.* New York: McGraw-Hill.
This book is a very helpful resource for those interested in creating and using structured input activities in their classrooms. The book is designed for audiences with little to no background in pedagogy. It uses devices for teachers to create their own structured input activities specific to their students' needs, addresses problematic areas when creating language activities, and presents research applicable to contemporary SLA methodology.

Lee, J. F., & VanPatten, B. (2003). *Making communicative language teaching happen* (2nd ed.). Boston: McGraw-Hill.

This text takes a comprehensive approach to communication within a classroom environment, with a particular focus on input-based approaches. It is aimed at teachers, teaching assistants, and education students who are looking to implement numerous strategies in their classrooms. This book gives numerous activities and tests designed to challenge learners.

VanPatten, B. (1996). *Input processing and grammar instruction in second language acquisition.* Norwood, NJ: Ablex Publishing Corporation.

This text provides an in-depth investigation of processing instruction. It focuses on the research behind the model, the potential challenges surrounding its use, its evolution, and how it works in contrast to traditional teaching methods. This is a useful handbook for understanding how input processing affects second language learning.

VanPatten, B. (2004). "Input processing in second language acquisition." In B. VanPatten (Ed.), *Processing instruction: Theory, research, and commentary* (pp. 5–31). Mahwah, NJ: Lawrence Erlbaum.

This text provides an in-depth investigation of processing instruction. However, unlike the 1996 version of this text, this edition contains contributions from other scholars with their views on the significance of this teaching method. For this reason, it would be excellent to use as a primary source because it gives a more balanced insight to this approach.

Chapter 3

Focus on Grammar through Textual Enhancement

Introduction

In the previous chapter, we examined processing instruction as an input-based approach to teaching grammar. The approach was concerned with raising learners' attention to grammatical forms through structured input activities whose aim was to alter learners' inappropriate processing strategies during comprehension. In this chapter, we will consider another input-based approach, namely, *textual enhancement*. The aim of this approach is to raise learners' attention to linguistic forms by rendering input perceptually more salient. Textual enhancement aims to achieve this by highlighting certain aspects of input by means of various typographic devices, such as *bolding*, *underlining*, and *italicizing* in written input, or acoustic devices such as *added stress* or *repetition* in oral input. The assumption is that such visual or phonological modifications of input make grammatical forms more noticeable and subsequently learnable.

The chapter is organized as follows. We begin by discussing the theoretical underpinnings of textual enhancement, with a focus on the notions of noticing and input enhancement. We will then discuss textual enhancement as an input enhancement technique and also the different ways in which it can be achieved, along with examples. Next, we will briefly review the empirical research that has examined the effectiveness of textual enhancement. The chapter will end with examples of activities that can be used in the classroom and a list of useful resources.

Theoretical Background

As discussed in the previous chapter, a crucial source of learning for L2 learners is input. However, SLA researchers have made a distinction between input and intake, defining input as the sample of the target language that learners are exposed to, and intake as what is registered in the learner's mind. It is intake that can be further processed and become part of the learner's developing language system.

However, the relationship between input and intake is not simple, and the fact that the learner is exposed to input does not necessarily guarantee that the input will become intake. Thus, the central question in theories of L2 acquisition has been how input turns into intake and how it will eventually lead to the development of L2 competence.

In answering these questions, many SLA researchers have examined the role of attentional processes in SLA and have found that intake does not take place until learners recognize what is in the input (Schmidt, 1990, 1993; Tomlin & Villa, 1994). It is this initial stage in learning that Schmidt (1990) has called *noticing*. In fact, Schmidt defined intake as "that part of the input that the learner notices" (p. 139). Gass and Selinker (2008) pointed out that "what is noticed ... interacts with a parsing mechanism which attempts to segment the stream of speech into meaningful units for the learner" (2008, p. 482).

Of course, the notion of noticing and attention is complex and, therefore, although there is agreement on its importance, disagreement exists on its exact definition and operationalization. For example, while Schmidt (1990) argued that learners' conscious awareness of linguistic forms is necessary for language learning, other researchers (e.g., Tomlin and Villa, 1994) have argued that conscious attention is not necessarily needed and that learners are able to acquire linguistic forms with minimum levels of, or even without, attention. For example, Tomlin and Villa (1994) argued that a more fine-grained analysis of the role of attention than that proposed by Schmidt is needed in order to explain how attention affects SLA processes. To this end, they distinguished among three separate but related attentional processes: *alertness*, *orientation*, and *detection*, and argued that what is essential for learning is detection. According to Tomlin and Villa, *alertness* concerns learners' readiness to receive the incoming stimuli. *Orientation* has to do with directing attentional resources to a particular type of input without paying attention to other input. *Detection* has to do with selection and registration of sensory stimuli in memory. To these researchers, it is the detected information that becomes available for other cognitive processes for learning, such as hypothesis formation and testing. In other words, it is the detected information that becomes intake. Tomlin and Villa proposed that detection can take place without any conscious awareness.

Although Schmidt originally argued that SLA does not take place without conscious attention, in more recent discussions (Schmidt, 2001), he has separated noticing and conscious awareness. He has argued that noticing can be limited to "awareness at a very low level of abstraction" (p. 5). Thus, in this revised version, Schmidt's notion of noticing is very close to that of detection put forth by Tomlin and Villa. Schmidt has also distinguished between noticing and understanding. Noticing is a process that involves simple mental registration of an event. Understanding, however, involves a deeper level of awareness, and pertains to processes such as recognition of general rules and principles.

However, despite controversies and differences in terminology, many SLA researchers agree that some level of attention is required for successful learning of linguistic forms (Carroll & Swain, 1993; Doughty, 2001; Doughty & Varela, 1998; Fotos, 1994; Fotos & Ellis, 1991; Nassaji, 1999; Nassaji & Fotos, 2004; Robinson, 1995; Schmidt, 1993, 2001; VanPatten, 2002b). Even for Tomlin and Villa, attention to input is a necessary process in SLA, even though they have ascribed less importance to awareness.

Input Enhancement

Given the centrality of the role of noticing, the question then becomes how to facilitate the noticing of a certain form. This is an important question because in naturalistic settings, not all features in the input are equally noticeable. Such considerations have led researchers to propose mechanisms that can help learners attend to aspects of input that may not be noticed under natural circumstances. In the previous chapter, we discussed processing instruction as one way of promoting learners' attention to form. Another way of enhancing noticeability of input is through increasing its perceptual salience. Perceptual salience refers to features of the target structure that are easily noticed. The process through which the salience of input is enhanced is called *input enhancement.*

The term input enhancement was first introduced by Sharwood Smith (1991). Sharwood Smith (1981) and Rutherford and Sharwood Smith (1985) originally used the term *consciousness-raising* rather than *input enhancement.* Their motivation for using this concept was to argue against Krashen's (Krashen, 1981, 1985) view that formal instruction plays little role in language learning. Rutherford and Sharwood Smith (1985, p. 274) opposed this view: "We will … question a current assumption that formal grammar has a minimal or even non-existent role to play in language pedagogy and that theoretical linguistics has virtually nothing to contribute to what goes on in the classroom."

They further noted:

> Instructional strategies which draw the attention of the learner to specifically structural regularities of the language, as distinct from the message content, will under certain conditions significantly increase the rate of acquisition over and above the rate expected from learners acquiring that language under natural circumstances where attention to form may be minimal and sporadic.

Although in their original discussions, Sharwood Smith and Rutherford used the notion of *consciousness-raising,* Sharwood Smith reconsidered the use of this term in his later publications. He argued that the term is misleading because it implies that learners' internal attentional mechanisms can be controlled or manipulated by the input, which is not true. Sharwood Smith prefers input enhancement as it is more accurate and suggests that what is controlled is external to the learner and can only be restricted to the materials presented. In other words, it limits the focus of intervention to drawing learners' attention to form through external operations carried out on input rather than to the manipulation of learners' internal processes. This is an important distinction because it suggests that external manipulations of input do not have any direct relationship to learners' internal processes. In other words, it is possible that input may be physically conspicuous but the learner may not become conscious of it. In such cases, enhancing input may not affect learning.

Of course, as Polio (2007) noted, the term consciousness-raising has continued to be used by many SLA researchers in the field of L2 teaching and learning. For example, both Fotos (1993) and Fotos and Ellis (1991) have used this term in their approach to teaching grammar. In particular, these researchers have advocated the use of consciousness-raising tasks in communicative language classrooms, considering it useful in drawing learners' attention to form. However, the way they have used consciousness-raising is similar to Sharwood-Smith's input enhancement. R. Ellis (1993b), for example, used the term consciousness-raising to refer to activities that help learners to understand a particular grammatical form and how it works (see Chapter 6).

Types of Input Enhancement

As noted earlier, input enhancement is the process by which input is made more noticeable to the learner. This can take different forms in pedagogical contexts, which can vary along at least two basic dimensions. Sharwood Smith (1991) called these dimensions *explicitness* and *elaboration*. Explicitness concerns the degree of directness in how attention is drawn to form. Elaboration has to do with the duration or intensity with which enhancement procedures take place. Explicit enhancement may be overt form-focused intervention in which the teacher explicitly directs learners' attention to particular linguistic features through various forms of metalinguistic explanation and rule presentation. Implicit enhancement occurs when learners' attention is drawn to grammatical forms while their main focus is on meaning. This may take the form of an indirect clue, such as a visual gesture to indicate an error in learners' production. Similarly, enhancement may vary in terms of intensity or elaboration. For example, at one end of the elaboration continuum, it may take the form of repeated explanation or correction of an error over an extended period of time. At the other end, it may take the form of a brief or single explanation of correction. According to Sharwood Smith, when combined, these two dimensions can create four types of enhancement techniques (Table 3.1).

Another distinction is between positive and negative enhancement (Sharwood Smith, 1991). Positive input enhancement refers to those strategies that make a correct form salient, thus, highlighting what is correct in the language. This has been referred to as *positive evidence* in the SLA literature. An example would be using stress to highlight a given correct form in the input. In such cases "if the learner has a different perception of the L2 grammar than is evidenced by the input, then positive evidence may serve as a trigger to change that

Table 3.1 Matrix of Enhancement Techniques

	Less explicit	*More explicit*
Less elaborate	Signal once when error occurs	Short explanation once when error occurs
More elaborate	Short signal each time error occurs	Long explanation each time error occurs

Source: Sharwood Smith (1991, p. 120).

grammar and bring it in line with the native-speaker grammar" (Sharwood Smith, 1991, pp. 122–23). Negative input enhancement highlights "given forms as incorrect, thus signaling to the learner that they have violated the target norms" (p. 177). An example of this would be the use of corrective feedback.

Input enhancement can also vary depending on whether it is achieved internally or externally (Sharwood Smith, 1991). Internal enhancement occurs when the learner notices the form himself or herself through the outcome of internal cognitive processes or learning strategies. For example, the learner may notice a grammatical feature as a way of processing input for meaning, such as paying more attention to content words than function words. External enhancement occurs when the form is noticed through external agents, such as the teacher or external operations carried out on the input.

Textual Enhancement as an External Input Enhancement Technique

Textual enhancement is an external form of input enhancement, by which learners' attention is drawn to linguistic forms through physically manipulating certain aspects of the text to make them easily noticed. Since the technique highlights the correct form in the input, it is a positive form of input enhancement. Textual enhancement is also an implicit form of input enhancement as it attempts to draw learners' attention to form while focus remains on meaning. In the previous chapter, we discussed processing instruction, which can also be considered a form of input enhancement. However, textual enhancement is different from processing instruction in that textual enhancement attempts to make forms salient in the input, whereas processing instruction tries "to provide opportunities for consistent form-meaning mappings in activities" (VanPatten, 1996, p. 84). Processing instruction is usually combined with direct instruction, thus providing an explicit form of input enhancement. However, textual enhancement does not involve any explicit instruction. Thus, learners' attention is drawn to forms implicitly and unobtrusively. Also, since textual enhancement involves highlighting forms in meaning-bearing texts, it meets the requirement of a focus on form approach, which maintains "meaning and use must already be evident to the learner at the time that attention is drawn to the linguistic apparatus needed to get the meaning across" (Doughty and Williams, 1998, p. 4).

Different Forms of Textual Enhancement

Textual Enhancement in Written Text

Textual enhancement can be used with both written and oral texts. In written text, this can be accomplished by typographically highlighting certain target words embedded in the text by means of textual modifications, such as *underlining, boldfacing, italicizing, capitalizing, color coding* or a combination of these. For example, students can be presented with a reading comprehension text, in which grammatical forms that the teacher identifies as problematic are highlighted using one or more of the above devices. The text can either be an authentic text, if it contains enough examples of the targeted form, or it can be modified for that purpose. However, as Wong (2005) cautioned, teachers should avoid highlighting many different target structures in the text because this would negatively affect the meaning process.

In textual enhancement, learners should read the text for meaning. Therefore, it is essential that the teacher use strategies that can keep learners' attention on message. This can be achieved by using various forms of post-reading activities. For example, the teacher can ask learners to read the text and then discuss its content with their peers, answer questions about the information in the text, or even complete a table or a chart based on the information in the text. The teacher should not explain why certain forms are highlighted in the input and should not provide any additional metalinguistic information either.

In summary, when designing textually enhanced texts, the following steps should be taken:

1   Select a particular grammar point that you think your students need to attend to.
2   Highlight that feature in the text using one of the textual enhancement techniques or their combination.
3   Make sure that you do not highlight many different forms as it may distract learners' attention from meaning.
4   Use strategies to keep learners' attention on meaning.
5   Do not provide any additional metalinguistic explanation.

The following provides an example of an enhanced text. The target form is the third person singular verbs in English. Each instance of the target form has been highlighted using the bold type.

Example (1)

> The man **goes** with his dog to the park. He **brings** a ball with him to throw for the dog. When he **arrives** at the park, he **throws** the ball very far, and the dog **chases** after it. The dog **comes** back with the ball in his mouth. The man **is** very happy to see the dog come back with the ball. He **spends** the rest of the day throwing the ball for his dog to chase.

Textual Enhancement in Oral Texts

Textual enhancement can also be used with oral texts. Oral input can be made more noticeable through various intonational and phonological manipulations, such as added stress, intonation, or repetitions of the targeted form, or even through gestures, body movement, or facial expressions.

For example, if students have problems with a certain target form, such as definite articles in English, the teacher can highlight those features when interacting with students by using added stress or repetition in his or her speech. Repetition is a useful textual enhancement device because it not only makes a certain form perceptually salient but it also allows the learner to have a longer time to process the incoming input. Hence it may cause the learner to better notice the targeted form.

The following from Nassaji (2007b, p. 59) illustrates an example of enhanced oral input during student–teacher interaction. In this example, the learner has made an error in the use of the past tense of *catch* during his conversation with the teacher. The teacher has reformulated the learner's error and has enhanced it with an added stress and rising intonation.

Example (2)

STUDENT: And she catched her.
TEACHER: She CAUGHT her? [*Enhanced with added stress*]
STUDENT: Yeah, caught her.

Another example of oral textual enhancement can be seen in Doughty and Varela's (1998, p. 124) study of focus on form. In this example, the teacher has enhanced the salience of the target forms through repetition of the learners' erroneous utterance followed by a correct reformulation with added stress.

Example (3)

JOSÉ: I think that the worm will go under the soil.
TEACHER: I *think* that the worm *will* go under the soil? [*Enhanced with repetition*]
JOSÉ: (no response)
TEACHER: I *thought* that the worm *would* go under the soil.
JOSÉ: I *thought* that the worm *would* go under the soil.

Input Flood

Another form of input enhancement is an *input flood*. In this technique, learners are provided with numerous examples of a certain target form in the input (either oral or written). The assumption here is that frequent instances of the same target form make it perceptually salient, drawing the learners' attention to form. The notion of input frequency and its effects on language acquisition has been examined in SLA research and has been proposed as an important factor in increasing the salience of targeted forms (e.g., N. Ellis, 2002; N. Ellis & Schmidt, 1998; Gass & Selinker, 2008). Gass and Selinker noted "[s]omething which is very frequent in the input is likely to be noticed" (2008, p. 482). Another benefit of input flood is that it provides the learner with ample exposure to the target form. Since this technique does not involve any direct intervention, it also provides an implicit method of focus on form.

Creating input flood tasks are easy. For example, if the intention is to make a certain particular feature salient, an oral or a written story can be used or constructed that contains many instances of that form. However the level of the input presented should be appropriate for the learner's level of language proficiency (Wong, 2005). As will be noted in Chapter 8, language proficiency is an important factor that needs to be considered when designing focus on form activities because if the activity is beyond learners' ability level, it may not be effective. Also as noted in the previous chapter, for learners to be able to attend to linguistic forms in the meaningful input, they need to be able to process the text at a minimal attentional cost. Thus, if the text is too difficult or contains too many difficult words, it may make the text incomprehensible. In such cases, even if the learner notices the target form, he or she may not be able to create the kind of form-mapping required for its acquisition.

The following provides an example of an input flood task. The target forms are the English definite and indefinite articles. Thus, the text has been designed to include numerous instances of those forms. It should be noted that in the input flood the target items should not be typographically highlighted.

Example (4)

> A chipmunk sat on some branches in a great big tree. It was very hungry, so it decided to leave the tree and look for food. It climbed off the branches and reached the trunk of the tree, and went down the trunk to the ground below. The chipmunk saw lots of grass, and in the grass lay many acorns! The chipmunk, in its delight, took as many acorns as it could, put them in its mouth, and ran back up the tree trunk to its nest. There, the chipmunk had a very good meal.

Effectiveness of Textual Enhancement

Now that we have presented textual enhancement techniques and examples, we can discuss their effectiveness. There are a number of studies that have examined the effectiveness of textual enhancement and input flood in L2 learning. Such studies have investigated types of enhancement, the nature of input, the cognitive processing involved in input processing, and their effects on both noticing and learning. In what follows, we will briefly review samples of such studies and their conclusions.

One of the studies that examined the effects of textual enhancement (Jourdenais et al., 1995) investigated whether or not textual enhancement had any effects on noticing and learners' processing of target forms. Two groups of Spanish learners were assigned to an enhancement group and a comparison group respectively. The enhancement group received a text in which instances of the target forms (Spanish preterite and imperfect verbs) were typographically highlighted; the enhancement group received the same text with no enhancement. The learners who received the enhanced text outperformed those who received the unenhanced text in both noticing and subsequent production of the target forms. Alanen (1995) examined the effects of textual enhancement versus explicit instruction on the acquisition of Finnish locative features and consonant gradation. Four groups of learners participated in the study: a group that received textual enhancement only, a group that received explicit instruction, a group that received both types of treatment, and a group that did not receive any treatment. The study found that the textual enhancement group benefited most from the treatment. However, the group who received explicit instruction outperformed the group who did not receive such instruction.

White (1998) examined the effects of textual enhancement on learning third person singular possessives in English among French-speaking children. The study involved 10 hours of instruction in which learners were exposed to textually enhanced target forms in their reading activities. It found that textual enhancement promoted noticing of the target forms but did not have a significant effect on developing learners' knowledge of the target structures.

A more recent study (Simard, 2009) investigated the effects of different forms of textual enhancement on learners' learning of English plural markers among grade eight French-speaking learners. The results showed that the effects of textual enhancement varied depending on the target form and the number of enhancements. Textual enhancement was most effective when a combination of formats was used. This study suggests that different forms of textual enhancement may have different effects on L2 learning.

Trahey and White (1993) examined the effects of input flood. The target form was adverb placement in French. Learners received two weeks of input flood tasks that contained frequent instances of the adverb. They found that the input flood helped learners to learn the new form but had limited effects on enabling them to identify errors in the target language. Williams and Evans (1998) examined the effects of input flood with two levels of explicitness: implicit (frequent instances of the target structure) and more explicit (flooding plus explicit instruction). Two target structures were examined: English participial adjectives and passive voice. The study showed that the effectiveness of textual enhancement varies depending on its degree of explicitness and type of the target form.

In summary, studies examining the effectiveness of textual enhancements including input flood have shown varying results, from positive and facilitative effects to limited and even no effects. While most of the studies suggest an overall positive effect for such techniques on noticing, they do not provide proof of learning. As Han, Park, and Combs (2008, p. 612) noted, part of the reason for these mixed results is because of methodological differences in research, which then limits the generalizability of the findings. In their review of a number of textual enhancement studies, they arrived at the following conclusions:

1   Simple enhancement is capable of inducing learner noticing of externally enhanced forms in meaning-bearing input.
2   Whether or not it also leads to acquisition depends largely on whether the learner has prior knowledge of the target form.
3   Learners may automatically notice forms that are meaningful.
4   Simple enhancement is more likely to induce learner noticing of the target form when sequential to comprehension than when it is concurrent with comprehension.
5   Simple enhancement of a meaningful form contributes to comprehension.
6   Simple enhancement of a non-meaningful form does not hurt comprehension.
7   Simple enhancement is more effective if it draws focal rather than peripheral attention.
8   Compound enhancement is more likely to induce deeper cognitive processing than enhancement, possibly to the extent of engendering "overlearning."

The above conclusions are not surprising as textual enhancement simply provides learners with correct models of the language (or what has been called *positive evidence*) not information with what is incorrect in the input (or what has been called *negative evidence*). Both types of evidence are essential and play an important role in L2 learning.

Classroom Activities: Additional Examples of Textual Enhancement

The following provides additional examples of textually enhanced texts for classroom purposes. The target forms have been enhanced through a combination of different textual enhancement devices such as *underlining, italicizing,* and *bolding.*

Activity I

Instruction: Please read the text and then answer the following questions.

A girl decided to go *cycling* for the day. She called her friends and asked them if they would be interested in *joining* her. They thought that *biking* would be an *exciting* thing to do on such a hot day. The girl and her friends took their bikes up a steep road, and went *flying* down the big hill. Many hours later, they finished *having* their fun and went home again.

Questions

1 Why did the girl call her friends?
2 Where did they go biking?
3 Did they enjoy biking?

Activity 2

Instruction: Please read the following text. Then in groups of two, discuss the following questions:

The teacher **has told** me that I have homework today. It will have to be completed by tomorrow. I **have looked** at it, and it looks very difficult. I have asked my brother if he **has** ever **worked** on homework like this. He **has** never **seen** an assignment like this before. This will be the first time that I **have needed** help!

Questions for Discussion

1 Has anything like this ever happened to you as a student?
2 What do you think the problem with the student's homework has been?
3 Do you think homework is useful?
4 Do you think homework will help learners to study harder?

Conclusion

In this chapter, we examined textual enhancement as a technique to draw learners' attention to grammatical forms in the input. However, although textual enhancement may promote noticing, it alone may not be able to bring about learning. Thus, to be most effective, textual enhancement needs to include more explicit forms of enhancement including various forms of input- and output-based practices and corrective feedback. As Batstone (1994) noted, if learners want to learn grammar effectively, they have to "act on it, building it into their working hypothesis about how grammar is structured" (p. 59). This may not happen unless learners are exposed to ample opportunities for noticing as well as producing the target form. Furthermore, although textual enhancement is easy to create and use, one shortcoming is that it is not always clear which forms should be highlighted in the text (Wong, 2005). Of course, through practical experience, teachers may have a good idea of which forms learners may have difficulty with at certain levels of language learning. However, it is still possible that not all learners have problems with the same target forms, or if they do, it is not clear whether they benefit from the same technique. Thus, like other focus on form strategies, textual enhancement should be seen as only one technique and should always be used in conjunction with other focus on form strategies. In general, input enhancement can become more effective if it is preceded by a formal mini-lesson on the target grammar structure and followed by a wrap-up, summarizing the target structure's use in the lesson. This would solidify learners' ability to notice and then process the target form.

Questions for Reflection

1 Textual enhancement is a form of implicit input enhancement. Discuss at least five possible reasons for using such implicit techniques in L2 classrooms.
2 Consider the difference between an input flood and explicit grammar instruction. What do you think are the advantages and disadvantages of each? What are some of the factors that may influence your choice between the two?
3 In this chapter we recommended that the teacher should not explain why certain forms are highlighted in a textually enhanced text. What do you think are the reasons for this advice?
4 Most of the studies that have used textual enhancement have found that this technique may help learners notice the target structure, but it does not necessarily bring about learning. What modifications do you think should be made to the textual enhancement technique so that it would be more effective for SLA?
5 In this chapter we also discussed input flooding as a kind of input enhancement technique. Have you had any experience with this technique in your classroom? If so, have you found it effective? If not, what modifications do you make to this technique to become effective?

Useful Resources

Gascoigne, C. (Ed.) (2007). *Assessing the impact of input enhancement in second language education*. Stillwater, OK: New Forums Press.
    The authors in this book look at the repercussions of enhancing the input for L2 learners. It examines consciousness-raising and input enhancement through the research of several experts in the field of SLA. It is useful to those who are looking for more than one approach to teaching methods.

Schmidt, R. (2001). "Attention." In P. Robinson (Ed.), *Cognition and second language instruction* (pp. 3–32). Cambridge: Cambridge University Press.
    This section discusses the relevance of attention to SLA, and its significance in relation to every aspect of second language learning. The chapter takes a

psychological stance in its explanation of attention as pivotal for SLA, and the argument that attention is necessary for L2 learning. This is useful for those who want to gain an understanding of the role of attention and its implications in L2 learning.

Sharwood Smith, M. (1991). "Speaking to many minds: On the relevance of different types of language information for the L2 learner." *Second Language Research, 72,* 118–32.
This paper looks at input enhancement and consciousness-raising in second language learning. It specifically examines input salience and how this can affect a language learner's competence and performance in communication. This is useful as an overview of the process by which input can become salient, and suggests how salience can be both a coincidental occurrence or a deliberate manipulation of the input in order for a specific feature to become activated in a learner's mental grammar.

Wong, W. (2005). *Input enhancement: From theory and research to the classroom.* New York: McGraw-Hill.
The writer provides a detailed description of the many different types of input enhancement, and targets an audience comprised mainly of inexperienced and/or beginning second language instructors. This book gives a detailed explanation of how influential input is for learner development, and what measures can be taken to further enhance awareness of grammatical form.

Chapter 4

Focus on Grammar through Discourse

Introduction

In this chapter we will consider the use of discourse to draw learners' attention to L2 target forms. A discourse-based pedagogy differs from other approaches to language teaching in that it not only focuses on grammar forms, but it also considers the meaning and use of those forms within the larger discourse context. As discussed in Chapter 1, centuries of structural/grammar-translation approaches to language teaching treated grammar as a sentence-level phenomenon consisting of a determined order of forms, usually studied through parsing, which established the rules for sentence construction. Whereas structural approaches to L2 teaching have traditionally emphasized instruction on grammar alone, recent approaches to language teaching have become more context-based. Thus, approaches to teaching grammar that focus on the form-meaning relationships of language have become popular (R. Ellis, 2006). Although still considering the importance of attention to linguistic forms, a discourse-based approach to teaching grammar considers its function to convey meaning. Thus, it deals with:

> not only the possible realizations in grammar of particular speech act functions such as requesting and suggesting (and their mitigation for reasons of politeness and tact), but the way in which grammatical categories such as tense, aspect and modality pattern across texts, the role of grammar in creating textual cohesion (reference, substitution, conjunction, etc.) and information structure (through devices of thematization such as adverbial placement, the use of the passive and clefting).
>
> (Trappes-Lomax, 2004, p. 154)

In the light of the above, we recognize that an essential function of grammar is its pragmatic meaning in context. As Widdowson (1978) suggested, the parts of a text or speech that learners must understand are discourse-based, consisting of: (1) the form of the text/speech; (2) the proposition, or what is being written/said; and (3) the illocutionary force, or the actual functional/pragmatic intent of the speaker/writer within a particular context. A fourth component, the act, is the function which is actually performed by the speech or text (e.g., "I now pronounce you man and wife" performs the act of marriage).

In this chapter, we examine how we can use the principles from a discourse-based approach to teaching language and how they can be applied to teaching grammar. We begin by examining the emergence of discourse-based L2 teaching, considering the argument for the use of discourse and the development of discourse competence in a FonF approach to grammar instruction. This is especially necessary in light of the fact that major standardized English proficiency tests such as the TOEFL have been revised to contain extensive discourse-based question items. We review recent developments in discourse-based instruction, including corpus linguistics, classroom discourse analysis, and the differences between the grammar of spoken and written discourse. Finally, we examine sample classroom applications of discourse-based form-focused instruction and present classroom activities.

What Are Discourse and Discourse Competence?

Discourse has been defined as "a continuous stretch of ... language larger than a sentence, often constituting a coherent unit" (Crystal, 1992, p. 25). Thus, a discourse-based pedagogy does not focus on grammar forms in isolation or simply at the sentence level, but attempts to integrate them into larger interactive contexts. The aim of this approach is to develop *discourse competence*, defined as the ability to process and create coherent discourse, and to argue for the necessity of moving beyond a sentence-level analysis of utterances to analyzing language as unified discourse (Bachman, 1990; Canale & Swain, 1980). A discourse-based approach treats grammar functionally (Trappes-Lomax, 2004) and holds a meaning-based view of grammar.

One of the major researchers within a meaning-based discourse view of grammar is Halliday (Halliday, 1978, 1984, 2004), who developed the theory of systematic functional grammar (SFG). SFG views grammar as a tool to achieve communicative goals through expressing particular meanings according to the requirements of the context (Halliday & Matthiessen, 2004). From this perspective, grammar is regarded as a complex process of making context-based choices, not only of syntax or vocabulary, but also considering social and psychological factors determined by the grammatical links between discourse and meaning (Halliday, 1978). Because of this complexity, it is not surprising that most researchers insist that the presentation of isolated grammar rules and the provision of sentence-level examples are insufficient for effectively teaching L2 grammar (see Edlund, 1995, p. 98). Halliday's systemic linguistic approach states that teachers need to consider language in its entirety "so that whatever is said about one aspect is to be understood always with reference to the total picture" (Halliday & Matthiesson, 2004, p. 19). Bruce (2008) further argues that the development of discourse competence is central to language teaching, so skills must be taught through discourse. In this chapter, we make a similar argument for teaching the four skills through a grammar-based approach.

Sentence-Level Versus Discourse-Level Grammar

The discourse view of language focuses less on analysis of the grammatical structure and more on analysis and description of "the interaction between [the] linguistic form ... and pragmatic conditions" (Tomlin, 1994, p. 145). It suggests that implicit or explicit instruction should be supported by the provision of discourse-level input to expose learners to repeated use of target forms in natural input. Learner discourse-level output producing target forms are also essential to promote learner noticing and ultimate acquisition of the target structures. This process is especially essential for today's language learners since most institutional tests now present listening, speaking and writing questions at the discourse level, often requiring learners to synthesize both written and spoken items when producing their answers.

An important distinction is also made between grammar as syntax and grammar as language use. Grammar as syntax refers to the ways in which words are arranged in a phrase, a clause, or a sentence and the rules governing these arrangements. Grammar as language use, however, refers to the ability to understand and use grammar in communicative discourse. Thus, a discourse-based view of language teaching emphasizes the communicative use of grammar, suggesting that learners must comprehend what is actually being communicated, regardless of the apparent meaning of the syntax. For example, when someone riding on a bus or train asks a person who is seated and has put his or her bag on the next seat, "Is this seat taken?" the speaker is requesting that the bag be moved in order to sit down, and does not expect the answer, "No, it isn't," although it would be syntactically correct. In this example, syntax does not convey the actual meaning of the utterance, and the learner must understand the communicative context.

Thus, grammar must be presented flexibly as a tool to achieve communicative goals through expressing particular meaning, cohesion and coherence according to the requirements of the context. From the discourse perspective, grammar is therefore the complex process of making context-based choices of syntax, vocabulary, and the social and psychological variables necessary for the intended meaning to be conveyed (Edlund, 1995, p. 98; see also McCarthy, 1991 on cohesion and coherence).

The Need for a Discourse-Based Focus on Grammar Teaching

In 1988, Rutherford outlined four possible positions regarding the relationship between grammar structure and function in L2 pedagogy (Rutherford, 1988, p. 231):

1   Grammar teaching is structural only, with no functional focus.
2   It is grammar-based and has a functional focus.
3   It is functional and has a grammar focus.
4   It is functional without any grammar focus.

There is strong empirical support for a view combining Rutherford's second and third options: L2 grammar instruction, either explicit or implicit, should take place in extended contexts rather than in isolation, and should include opportunities for learners to receive meaningful input and to produce meaningful output containing the target form, as mentioned in the introductory chapter. This recommendation is based on research from the 1990s indicating, as discussed previously, that purely communicative approaches have failed to produce target-like accuracy and that grammar instruction is therefore essential. Such research has produced renewed interest in formal grammar instruction, but of a very different nature than that found in traditional structural approaches.

A key concept in the cognitive theories of FonF is the importance of frequency of learner exposure to a target item (Long & Robinson, 1998). Research findings (Biber & Reppen, 2002; N. Ellis, 2002, 2007) indicate that learners must encounter target structures repeatedly in discourse-level contexts until a certain threshold of encounters is reached, at which point the form often becomes incorporated into learners' interlanguage system. N. Ellis (2002) has commented that until quite recently the tendency to ignore the importance of frequency in L2 acquisition has been erroneously derived from the association of frequency with behaviorism. However, corpus research has established the importance of frequency of exposure to target items as a critical and essential aspect of successful SLA (Levy, 1997). It is now acknowledged that learners need to acquire chunks of speech, formulaic utterances, and frequently occurring collocations through communicative usage. Only discourse-level input can provide learners with repeated authentic examples of these important forms and only discourse-level output can give learners the necessary chances to produce the new forms.

Research on L2 learner attitudes also provides support for a discourse-based FonF approach. A number of studies suggest that learners prefer pedagogical grammar explanations to structural explanations, and that the real-life examples of contextualized grammar forms provided in pedagogical grammars were particularly noticed by the learners (Berry, 2004). Some authors have even written grammar-based lesson texts based on humor (Woolard, 1999) to promote learners' positive emotional response to grammar study. Even research on grammar teaching for English native speakers (summarized in Weaver, 1996, pp. 179–80) indicates that studying grammar as an isolated system is less effective than when instruction is combined with multiple exposures to meaningful contexts such as extensive reading, learner writing (especially journal writing for extensive writing practice), self-correction of essays, and listening and speaking opportunities.

Consequently, there has been a recent rise of discourse-level, meaning-based views of L2 instruction (e.g., Butler, 2003; Celce-Murcia & Olshtain, 2001; R. Ellis, 2003; Hinkel, 2004; Larsen-Freeman, 2001) that advocate teaching L2 grammar through discourse-level contexts such as listening to extended dialogues and talks, watching movies and videos, having meaning-focused conversations, doing multi-paragraph readings and writing essays and journals. Researchers have also pointed out that many discourse-level communicatively based resources, with grammatical, lexical and phonological support, are now available online (Warschauer, 2004) to be used inside of class or outside for learners' self-study.

Although still structure-based, many pedagogical grammars now provide functional introductions to the structural presentation of grammar points, emphasizing use of the target forms in communication. For example, chapter titles in teacher training texts often link form and function, such as "Expressing judgments and attitudes: Modal auxiliaries and modality" (Lock, 1996, p. vii). Popular ESL/EFL grammar textbooks, though usually organized according to structures, often present new material on the basis of their function, for example "Making logical conclusions: Must" (Azar, 2003, p. 210), or "Stative Verbs: A Visit to the Doctor" (R. Ellis & Gaies, 1999, p. 11). Current multi-dimensional ESL/EFL textbooks (Nunan, 2001; Richards, 2003) usually organize their syllabus by communicative functions and topics, although sections providing explicit rule-based grammar instruction, examples and conversation practice opportunities are included in each lesson. Often these books contain a CD with discourse-level listening exercises that learners can study by themselves or as a group in the media center.

Despite these developments, traditional structural approaches still continue to be a common unit of organization in classroom material. For this reason, pedagogical grammars have been criticized by a number of researchers (Hunston & Gill, 1998) for their lack of innovation. For the most part, they are still characterized by the presentation of simple rules about structures and sentence-level exemplification of their use, even in conversation exercises.

Corpus Linguistics and a Focus on Grammar

Corpus linguistics, a term first appearing in the early 1980s (McEnery, Xiao, & Tono, 2006) is the study of language as expressed in corpora or large bodies of text. Recently the term *corpus* has been defined as "a collection of sampled texts, written or spoken, in machine-readable form which may be annotated with various forms of linguistic information" (McEnery et al., 2006, p. 4). Biber, Conrad, and Reppen (1998, p. 4) describe the essential characteristics of corpus analysis as follows: (a) it is empirical, analyzing the actual patterns of use in natural texts; (b) it utilizes a large and principled collection of natural texts, known as a "corpus" as the basis for analysis; (c) it makes extensive use of computers for analysis, using both automatic and interactive techniques; and (d) it depends on both quantitative and qualitative analytical techniques.

In the past, the only way to analyze text-based language was to read the texts and write down all instances of the target structure, a time-consuming process. For example, the first *Oxford English Dictionary* was compiled over decades in the late 19th century (and was fully published only in 1928) by examination and collation of thousands of slips of paper, each containing a quotation with a target lexical item (Scott & Tribble, 2006). However, in the 1960s, linguists began to use computers to create corpora for text analysis and the first electronic corpus, the million-word Brown Corpus of Standard American English, was developed at this time.

For decades, corpora have been used extensively to develop vocabulary lists (Godwin-Jones, 2001) and, with the increasing accessibility of concordancing software, "concordances" or lists of usages of the target term, are now used by L2 learners to examine patterns of target language usage and their frequencies in natural discourse. Items studied include vocabulary (especially the identification of key words in bodies of text on the basis of frequency), collocations (including the *node* or target word, and its *collocates*, the words which co-occur with the node), syntax, cohesion, metaphor, connotation, register, nuances of differences between synonyms, stylistic rules, and usages contradicting prescriptive grammar rules. Lexical errors have been found to be the most prevalent learner error and are the most significant barrier to effective communication, so it has been suggested that corpus searches can clarify lexical items and their use in written and spoken communication (Grander & Tribble, 1998). Corpora have also been used to analyze the unique features of particular text or spoken genre such as register, academic English, media discourse, legal discourse and workshop discourse (McEnery et al., 2006).

Corpus linguistics has important implications for a discourse-based approach to L2 instruction in the areas of syllabus design, materials development and classroom activities. It provides an approach to language teaching that is supported by what has been termed *data-driven learning* (DDL) (see articles in Partington, 1998; Sinclair, 2004, and the special issue of *Language Learning and Technology* on L2 teaching with corpora). DDL has been defined as "the use in the classroom of computer-generated concordances to get students to explore regularities of patterning in the target language, and the development of activities and exercises based on concordance output" (Johns & King, 1991, p. iii). These activities will be discussed in more detail in subsequent sections.

It has also been suggested (Bernardini, 2004) that DDL provides opportunities for discovery learning since L2 learners are able to inductively generate grammar rules by considering the great number of examples supplied by a corpus search using concordancing software. Learner use of concordances is also suggested to promote critical thinking by discouraging an over-reliance on prescriptive grammar presentations and by encouraging a focus on the actual use and frequency of target items and the observed relationship between form and meaning.

DDL learning is also seen as an important resource for remedying the current mismatch between authentic target language usages, patterns, and frequencies of grammar structures and what is presented in most L2 textbooks. For example, many texts suggest that the most common use of the simple present tense is habitual and re-occurring ("I go to school every day"). However, corpus analysis indicates that this usage occurs only 5.5% of the time, whereas 57.7% of the usages is the actual present ("I see what you mean") or neutral time ("My name is Ann") (Tsui, 2004, p. 41). Since many textbook presentations of grammar structures do not reflect real-life usages, it has been strongly suggested (Biber & Reppen, 2002) that material developers should use corpus analysis to determine the frequencies of grammatical structures in authentic language and be careful to reflect these frequencies in the materials they design.

A 10-year corpus-based study of the English verb system (Mindt, 2002) is an example of the corpus-derived development of an English pedagogical grammar. The grammar is based on authentic texts and includes frequency counts, making it possible to distinguish common usages from less frequent occurrences. Geared to advanced L2 learners, this pedagogical grammar recommends new categories derived from corpus analysis, such as a new structural description of the English verb phrase distinguishing between finite and non-finite verbs. As with most corpus-based pedagogy for grammar teaching, this approach to grammar is inductive, moving from language data to grammatical descriptions and rule generation.

Another form of corpus-based grammar teaching deals with grammatical variation, asserting its importance in L2 teaching while noting that many practitioners seem to ignore variation when presenting grammar rules. However, when studied through corpus analysis, patterns of variation can be identified, such as shifts due to register changes and other pragmatic considerations. For example, although use of *though* as a linking adverbial occurs frequently in spoken corpus analysis, this function is usually ignored in grammar textbook presentations. Such a lack of corpus data on key structures leads to the omission of important functional considerations assisting learners to develop pragmatic competence.

A different approach to corpus-based L2 grammar teaching made use of learner corpora to identify areas of difficulty (Nesselhauf, 2004). Here the language produced by a group of L2 learners is compared with the language produced by native speakers, either by the learners themselves as a DDL activity, or through the use of material provided by the teacher. For example, the Longman Learner Corpus was used to identify common learner errors, and these were incorporated into the Longman Essential Activator (1997) with the correct forms placed in special "alert boxes." The same corpus was also used in the creation of the *Longman Dictionary of Common Errors* (Heaton & Turton, 1987).

Another approach has used corpus analysis of clusters, defined as words which follow each other in a text (Scott & Tribble, 2006, p. 131), such as "as a result of" or "the way in which," in the instruction of English for Academic Purposes to create word cluster lists of academic phrases for L2 writing.

Discourse Analysis and Grammar

Discourse analysis (DA) is concerned with the relationships between language forms and the context in which they are used. As defined by Harris in 1952, discourse analysis consists of identifying the structural patterns that form connections across sentences. However, identification of textual patterns does not necessarily indicate their meaning in communication, and pragmatic considerations are essential to make sense of the real function of the text or utterance. Following this consideration, Celce-Murcia and Olshtain (2001, p. 4) suggest that a piece of discourse is:

> an instance of spoken or written language that has describable internal relationships of form and meaning (e.g., words, structures, cohesion) that relate coherently to an external communicative function or purpose and a given audience/interlocutor.

Thus, the communicative function and the participants are prime considerations. However, in many cases, discourse analysis is not used for study of grammar usage but rather is aimed at investigating the nature of social interaction. There have been a number of publications summarizing what is known about English discourse (e.g., Kasper & Blum-Kulka, 2003; Schiffrin, Tannen, & Hamilton, 2001), and presenting discourse analysis as a sociocultural concern, focusing primarily on language use within minorities and speech communities or for pragmatic purposes. For example, most conversation analysis examines the behavior of the participants rather than the grammar structures used to convey meaning. Even when grammar is the main focus, as McCarthy noted, "How we interpret grammatical form depends on a number of factors, some linguistics, some purely situational" (1991, p. 7).

Another important implication of discourse analysis studies for a communicative focus on grammar is an examination of *connected speech* or discourse-length utterances (J. D. Brown & Kondo-Brown, 2006, p. 2) to study pronunciation, stress and intonation. Connected speech has been defined by Crystal (1980) as a continuous sequence of spoken language as contrasted with the study of isolated linguistic units, such as individual sounds, words, phrases or sentence stress. Many teachers feel that an appreciation of such aspects of speech cannot occur at the sentence level and must be taught and understood through form-focused discourse.

Functional approaches to language teaching (see the summary in McCarthy 1991) also emphasize teaching grammar as used for particular communicative functions such as ordering in a restaurant, shopping or talking on the telephone and the presentation of this type of material is common in textbooks, as noted above (Halliday, 1994).

The Grammar of Oral Versus Written Discourse

From a discourse-based perspective, there are significant differences between spoken and written grammar necessitating the meaning-focused presentation of target forms in both modalities to clarify structure–meaning relationships. The differences are summarized in Table 4.1 (G. Brown & Yule, 1994; Murray, 2000) (this summary of G. Brown & Yule, 1994, and Murray, 2000 is adapted from Fotos, 2004, pp. 112–13). These differences have important implications for teaching language forms through discourse, which will be described later in this section.

Many important insights into the differences between speech and writing have been provided by corpus linguistics. For example, based on the results of corpus analysis of a five-million-word spoken corpus, ten criteria for the creation of a spoken pedagogical grammar have been identified (McCarthy & Carter, 2002). These criteria include determination of the parts of a spoken grammar, recognition of phrasal complexity, the location of elements in a clause, and the existence of patterns in extended discourse. The *Longman Student Grammar of Spoken and Written English* (Biber et al., 1999) provides an extensive analysis of the grammar of spoken English, determining that speech is characterized by the following most frequent grammar structures:

Table 4.1 Differences between Spoken and Written Language

Spoken	Written
1 In spoken language, speakers usually take turns, so the length of each turn is relatively short.	1 Written language generally consists of unbroken discourse.
2 Most speech lacks formal discourse markers since the relationship between current and past speech often depends on the context of the talk.	2 Written language builds coherence by use of formal connecting forms such as "however" or "therefore," which show the relationship between different parts.
3 Speech has a simplified grammar and vocabulary.	3 Written language is usually in a standard and consistent form.
4 Speech vocabulary is often simplified, referring to previously discussed topics or shared information, and is characterized by ellipsis and anaphora.	4 Written vocabulary is often more complex, and is often characterized by complex morphological structures.
5 Speech is often accompanied by paralinguistic information such as body language, gestures, facial expression, etc.	5 Paralinguistic information is absent in written discourse.
6 Speech usually has considerable repetition and redundancy.	6 Written discourse rarely contains repetition and redundancy.
7 Speech uses multiple registers, sometimes within the same discourse.	7 Written discourse is more uniform in terms of register and standards of usage.

- questions, including the use of *do* as a pro-verb and wh-words for information questions;
- the pronouns *you* and *I*;
- contractions;
- present tense verbs;
- speech fillers;
- stative verbs such as *feel* or *believe*;
- negatives formed by adding *n't* to the auxiliary (or pro-verb *do*).

The frequencies of these forms in natural spoken language are different from those found in written English. In fact, the third edition (2003) of Leech and Svartvik's classic *A Communicative Grammar of English* now features a strong emphasis on the grammar of the spoken language to provide a better balance between written and spoken forms, in particular, the treatment of grammar functions in extended discourse.

Further research (Scott & Tribble, 2006) on the differences between speech and writing involves a corpus-based investigation of key words in four types of text: spoken English conversation, spoken academic English, written fiction, and written academic English, to illustrate the significant lexical, syntactic and semantic differences among written and spoken texts of different genres, and between informal and academic language usages.

Effective Use of Discourse-Based Activities in a Classroom Focus on Grammar

At this point, a fundamental question is how to make effective use of discourse in form-focused L2 classroom instruction. As discussed previously, language functions are linked to specific grammatical structures. Therefore, a discourse-based communicative focus on grammar strongly supports the development of teaching materials that consider characteristics of both written and spoken language. It has been repeatedly noted that ESL/EFL pedagogical grammars are based on the structure of written English, not on the structure of speech, even though the two forms have been shown to be quite different (Nunan, 1998). In particular, the provision of authentic spoken material is extremely problematic since most textbooks continue to use the grammar of written English even for dialogue-based activities. A significant example of this is the continued use of the sentence-level example in grammatical explanations of target structures, even though many corpus researchers now consider sentences to be minor units in discourse since many non-sentences are used in natural language. As one researcher noted in 1991 (McCarthy, 1991, p. 51), a major problem is that:

> [S]ome of the structural options frequently found in natural data are ignored or underplayed in language teaching ... probably owing to

the continued dominance of standards taken from the written code. If the desire is to be faithful, grammar teaching may have to reorient some of its structural descriptions.

It is now clear that discourse-level examples of instructed forms in the four major language skills (listening, speaking, reading and writing) are essential for grammar teaching. As researchers have recommended, grammar pedagogy should also emphasize that word-order choices, tense-aspect choices, and that the use of special grammatical constructions are pragmatic and context-related, necessitating learner comprehension and application of instructed grammar rules at the discourse level (Celce-Murcia & Olshtain, 2001; Liu & Master, 2003). Consequently, form-focused discourse is becoming increasingly used in newer ESL/EFL textbooks to teach the four L2 skills, as shown below.

Teaching the four language skills through discourse:

1 Reading extended texts rather than sentences and answering comprehension questions.
2 Listening to extended speech and often requiring the learner to "shadow" the speaker's voice, complete a cloze test afterwards, reconstruct the text (see Swain & Lapkin, 1998) and answer comprehension questions.
3 Writing at the essay level, producing an introduction, a body and a conclusion (see for example, Fotos & Hinkel, 2007).
4 Speaking activities such as presenting speeches, either prepared or impromptu, or making discourse-length responses to questions.

Classroom Activities

In the following sections we will discuss specific activities for both teachers and learners to show how discourse-level input and output can be used to focus on grammar in L2 classrooms. These activities combine form-focused instruction with the provision of discourse-level naturalistic input, exposing learners to repeated use of target forms. Discourse-level output producing target forms is also viewed as essential in promoting noticing and ultimate acquisition of the target structures and will be considered as well.

Activity 1. Teachers Exploring Authentic and Non-authentic Language Use

Because of the gap between written dialogues in L2 textbooks and real-life interaction, it has been recommended to use authentic materials, like those developed for L1 speakers, such as newspaper articles, fiction, transcripts of news programs or listening activities based on movie or TV dialogues. However, the use of authentic materials for L2 learners is often problematic because of the difficulty in preparing material, such as the need to transcribe recordings, and the fact that such material is often too advanced for beginning or intermediate level learners. An increasingly acceptable alternative has been to simplify authentic text by careful rewriting so that it matches the proficiency level of the L2 learners who will use it. Although some practitioners may object to the lack of authenticity of simplified materials, it is suggested (Day & Bamford, 1998) that such materials should be regarded as "authentic" since they represent an attempt to communicate with the target learners at a comprehensible level. However, learners should receive a mixture of authentic and simplified material, with both types supplying multiple uses of the target grammar structures. The following example by Nunan (1998) demonstrates the provision of learners with opportunities to explore grammatical relationships in both authentic and non-authentic texts, emphasizing that learners need a "balanced diet" of both types of text (p. 105).

Directions for the Students

Study the following extracts. One is a piece of genuine conversation, the other is taken from a language teaching textbook. Which is which? What differences can you see between the two extracts? What language do you think the non-authentic conversation is trying to teach? What grammar would you need in order to take part in the authentic conversation?

Text A	Text B
A: Excuse me, please. Do you know where the nearest bank is?	A: How do I get to Kensington Road?
B: Well, the City Bank isn't far from here. Do you know where the main post office is?	B: Well you go down Fullarton Road…
	A:… what, down Old Belair, and around…?
	B: Yeah. And then you go straight…
A: No, not really. I'm just passing through.	A:… past the hospital?
B: Well, first go down this street to the traffic light.	B: Yeah, keep going straight, past the racecourse to the roundabout. You know the big roundabout?
A: OK.	A: Yeah.
B: Then turn left and go west on Sunset Boulevard for about two blocks. The bank is on your right, just past the post office.	B: And Kensington Road's off to the right.
	A: What, off the roundabout?
	B: Yeah.
A: All right. Thanks!	A: Right.
B: You're welcome.	

Activity 2. Teachers Using Discourse-level Input and Output

Researchers (e.g., Hinkel, 2002; McNamara, Hill, & May, 2002) now recommend the use of discourse-level oral and written output rather than sentence-level output to assess learners' pragmatic competence and oral proficiency. As observed previously, this is reflected in the nature of standardized test questions that now require discourse production through speaking or essay writing.

Trappes-Lomax (2004, p. 154) suggests that "through grammar we create whenever we speak or write." According to him, when teaching grammar, we must attend to the lexico-grammatical features of the text, written or spoken, and attempt to discover various ways in which these features contribute to textual cohesion. This can be facilitated by considering the role of lexical and grammatical phrases in the text in relation to their discoursal functions. In this context, the author highlights the centrality of developing learners' discourse level receptive and productive skills. He proposes the following activities as a way of enhancing skills in these areas. For the receptive role, he suggests:

1 Activating appropriate knowledge structures (schemata), both formal (genre) and content (knowledge of the topic) through pre-listening/reading activities.
2 Foregrounding contextually relevant shared knowledge to help in predicting topic development and guessing speaker/writer intentions.
3 Devising tasks which promote appropriate use of top-down processing (from macro-context to clause, phrase, and lexical item) and bottom-up practicing.
4 Processing (from lexical item, phrase and clause to macro-context).
5 Focusing on meta-discoursal signaling devices.

(Trappes-Lomax, 2004, p. 155)

To enhance the productive roles, he suggests attention to the following areas:

1 Salient features of context (setting, scene, the predicted state of knowledge and expectations of the reader/hearer).
2 The means whereby a speaker or writer projects himself or herself as a certain kind of person, "a different kind in different circumstances" (Gee, 1999, p. 13).
3 Function (communicative goals); the "socially situated activity that the utterance helps to constitute" (Gee, 1999, p. 13).
4 Appropriate instrumentalities (features of register and genre).
5 Development of effective communication strategies appropriate to the mode of communication (Trappes-Lomax, 2004, p. 155).

Teachers can also promote discourse-length output through the use of communicative tasks (e.g., R. Ellis, 2003). There are different ways in which these two recommendations can be achieved in L2 classrooms. For example, e-mail exchange tasks have been used by a number of teachers (Fotos, 2004) as a way of providing learners with meaningful discourse-level output opportunities. Teachers can also require weekly submissions of daily life written journals to encourage discourse-level extensive writing (Day & Bamford, 1998). Use of the internet strongly supports this suggestion as there are numerous sites providing MP3 files to download and listen to, blog sites where learners can read and write blogs in the target language, pronunciation sites, "chat" sites, where students can talk online with one another through text or speech, and many other learning opportunities (see Fotos & Browne, 2004).

Activity 3. Having Students Write Discourse for Authentic Purposes

Directions for the Teacher

Intermediate to advanced level students can be requested to exchange weekly L2 e-mail with their classmates on their daily activities or similar themes. Over the course of a semester of regular e-mail exchange, it has been found that the number of words produced by L2 students greatly increases (Fotos & Hinkel, 2007) due to such regular communicative output opportunities.

Composition teachers can request students to submit a weekly journal consisting of several pages describing their general activities. These are read and commented on by the teacher, but not corrected since the focus is on content and the aim is to promote extensive writing.

Activity 4. Using Discourse-based Activity Templates

An important pedagogical format for combining deductive and inductive approaches for discourse-level contexts has come from Celce-Murcia (2002; Celce-Murcia & Larsen-Freeman, 2003, p. 92). Although this activity template was designed for teacher trainees, it could be used by high intermediate or advanced level learners as well.

Activity 5. An Activity Template

Ten steps to solve a usage problem in the L2:

1 Identify the usage problem.
2 Review what grammar texts and researchers have said about the problem.
3 Examine natural written/spoken discourse of native speakers for uses of the target form, considering the context and the reason for the choice of the form.
4 Develop a hypothesis about why the form was used.
5 Test the hypothesis with discourse analysis and/or elicitation techniques.
6 Consult language corpora to examine further examples of usage.
7 Look for grammatical relationships with other forms, collocations, and items that precede or follow the target form.

8 Examine the role of the target item in discourse; e.g., does it initiate or terminate episodes? Does it contribute to cohesion and coherence? Where does it occur in natural discourse?

9 Examine whether the target form reflects affective or social interactional features of the discourse.

10 Develop an activity that presents the usage in natural communication followed or preceded by a formal mini-lesson on the grammar structure.

Sample Student Activity Based on a Template

The following activity is designed for discourse-level learner reading. The text for this activity (Thornbury, 2005, pp. 129–31) comes from a charity brochure appealing for donations: Give a widowed mother a goat. The goat produces milk. The goat produces manure. The widow sells more crops. The goat produces more goats. The widow keeps a goat. The widow gives a goat back.

Beginning to intermediate students perform the following activities:

1 A warm-up session consisting of instructions which the learners must act out, similar to Total Physical Response.

2 Schemata activation, in which the teacher asks the learners what the most useful thing would be to give a widowed mother in Africa, then asks the learners to discuss this in groups.

3 The first reading of the text, where the learners read the text silently using their dictionaries.

4 Learner response to text by establishing the discourse function of the text and discussing the idea.

5 Questions from the teacher requiring learner scanning of the text.

6 Reconstructing the text by completing a text-based cloze activity.

7 A language focus section in which the learners are made aware of target structures in the text, such as articles and verb forms, through cloze activities and substitution exercises.

8 Learner pair work to write their own text. This and similar activities can be modified according to the level of the learners.

Activity 6. Discourse-based Comprehension Activities

An early example of a discourse-based comprehension approach is given in Widdowson's doctoral dissertation (1973). He notes that questions based on extended discourse enable learners to develop formal knowledge about the target structure and the circumstances of its use. They also provide numerous opportunities to notice the target structure in meaning-focused contexts and remain aware of it. He presents an exercise on rephrasing which requires the students to replace an expression in italics in a discourse passage with one which means the same thing, noting that the intention is to draw the learner's attention to the way meanings are dependent upon the discourse of which they form a part (Widdowson, 1973, p. 232).

Activity 7. Using Corpora to Encourage Learners to Focus on Grammar

As discussed above, the term *corpus* refers to a computerized database consisting of hundreds of millions of words of authentic texts and spoken transcripts, usually with the parts of speech tagged (POST). It is searched by a concordancer, a software program designed to analyze corpora for every occurrence of a key word or phrase, and to display the results either alphabetically or on the basis of frequency. This display is known as a *concordance* and it is usually presented in KWIC (key word in context) format in which every instance of the target structure is centered and bolded on a separate line with a number of words displayed before and after the item. The following concordance-based activity from Thornbury (1999, p. 66) shows an example of how to use concordances to help learners understand the correct uses of lexical items such as *remember, forget,* and *stop.* The number of examples shown has been cut to three each, but at least 12 is recommended to show the variety of usages.

Instructions

The teacher divides the class into three groups (A, B, and C), and gives each group a different set of concordance lines as shown below. The groups are told to study their lines, and divide them into two patterns. If they find this difficult, they should be told to look at the form of the verb that immediately follows the word in the central column of each set of lines and try to discover the differences. If possible, they should formulate a grammar rule.

Group A: Remember (19.26, 07.05.98)

Yanto, thoughtfully. On the other hand, **remember** seeing them dancing together at a ball shortly before the month's Top to Tail if you own a poodle. **Remember** to listen out for Katie and friends on Radio 2. Should you there wasn't anyone to see me go.   **remember** thinking how white and cold her face looked, with

Group B: Forget (18.53, 07.05.98)

government last year announced that those who   **forget** to flush public toilets will be fined
up to US dollars. Results frothy fronds lit up by evening sun. I'll never   **forget** seeing your Grandfather for the first
time. I couldn't believe acting inspector over the weekend. I'll never   **forget** being in hospital.

Group C: Stop (19.18, 07.05.98)

tense, listening. At the age of twelve, Bailey   **stopped** eating meat. Although he had already taken his first
mouthful though Anna was sure her mother had not **stopped** having baths or using perfume. Annabel was
determined asthma? And it was two o'clock when they   **stopped** talking, they stopped having their break! Results of
your

Thornbury (1999, p. 66)

Activity 8. Teachers Conducting Discourse Analysis of their Own Output

Researchers have often promoted discourse analysis as a tool for the L2 classroom to highlight cultural and pragmatic differences in language usage and functions (Hinkel, 1999, 2004; Rose & Kasper, 2001). This tool can also be used to assist grammar instruction. The teacher can conduct the following activity in order to increase his or her awareness of the impact of teacher classroom discourse on learner participation and language use.

Activity 9. Videotaping and Analyzing a Lesson

This activity involves videotaping and analyzing a lesson to observe the impact of their questions and classroom dialogue on learner participation.

Instructions for the Teacher

1 Videotape a complete lesson, including your questions and the students' responses. (Opportunities to speak the target language are often created by teachers' questions.)
2 Watch the videotape. As you watch it, think about the types of questions you asked. Look for recurring patterns in your questioning style and the impact it has on the students' responses.
3 Transcribe questions and other parts of the lesson. A transcript will make it easier to focus on the specific type of questions asked and student responses.
4 Analyze the videotape and transcript. Why did you ask each question? What type of question was it—open (e.g., "What points do you think the author was making in the chapter you read yesterday?") or closed (e.g., "Did you like the chapter?")? Was the question effective in terms of your goals for teaching and learning? What effect did your questions have on the students' opportunities to practice the target language? How did the students respond to different types of questions? Were you satisfied with their responses? Which questions elicited the most discussion from the students? Did the students ask any questions?

By focusing on actual classroom interaction, teachers can investigate how one aspect of their teaching style affects students' opportunities for speaking the target language. They can then make changes that will allow students more practice with a wider variety of discourse types. See http://www.cal.org/resources/Digest/0107demo.html.

Activity 10. Using Discourse-based Input Activities to Build a Sense of Cohesion and Coherence in Written and Spoken Text

A major focus of discourse analysis in L2 learning has been the study of cohesion, defined as the links between clauses and sentences in speech or writing. Teachers can choose an authentic piece of text and can request the students to examine how target grammar items create links across sentence boundaries. Students should focus on how words are related to create different patterns of usage.

Another area where discourse analysis has been used for L2 instruction is examination of coherence by considering top-down planning and organization in written discourse (McCarthy, 1991). The teacher can select a piece of text containing multiple uses of a target form, such as the definite article *the* Students are requested to examine the function of each use of *the* in the discourse, and then to analyze the context of its use, making generalizations about its occurrence, its meaning, and the circumstances of its use and non-use.

Conclusion

This chapter has considered recent changes in L2 classroom pedagogy regarding the relationship between grammatical structures and their discourse-level functions. The research and recommendations summarized here suggest that the provision of discourse-level input based on authentic or simplified target language discourse, the study of discourse-level communicative contexts in which L2 forms are used, and the provision of opportunities for form-focused discourse-level output can greatly support implicit and explicit grammar instruction and can promote increased learner awareness of grammar forms, this leading to successful SLA.

Questions for Reflection

1 What is discourse-based instruction? How does it differ from sentence-level instruction and why is it important for L2 acquisition?
2 What is the difference between written language and speech? Why is this important for materials design?
3 What do the findings from corpus studies on usage frequencies indicate about the traditional textbook presentation of grammar forms? What do some corpus researchers recommend?
4 Review Celce-Murcia's (Celce-Murcia & Larsen-Freeman, 2003, p. 92) steps for combining a deductive and inductive approach to grammar teaching. How can this be used to develop a lesson for your own teaching situation?
5 Create a lesson on reading authentic discourse, answering questions on the reading, and summarizing the reading in a few sentences. What is the advantage of such a lesson in promoting learner independence? How could concordancing be used to strengthen this lesson plan?

Useful Resources

Celce-Murcia, M., & Olshtain, E. (2001). *Discourse and context in language teaching: A guide for language teachers*. Cambridge: Cambridge University Press.

This is a useful book for those who wish to use discourse and pragmatics in their teaching to create communicative classrooms. Curriculum discourse development is also discussed, as is classroom research. Each chapter ends with discussion questions and classroom activities.

McKay, S. (2002). *Teaching English as an international language: Rethinking goals and approaches.* Oxford: Oxford University Press.
This is an excellent book analyzing standards for English in various cultural contexts, and suggesting a number of discourse-based curriculum designs and activities suitable for various international contexts and learners. McKay's section on target cultural materials is especially useful.

Thornbury, S. (2005). *Beyond the sentence: Introducing discourse analysis.* Oxford: Macmillan Publishers.
This is a useful book that presents grammar at a discourse level. *Beyond the sentence* contains a section with photocopyable worksheets involving discourse-level tasks such as classifying target forms in terms of their function, or comparing and answering questions on texts.

Thornbury, S. (2006). *Grammar.* Oxford: Oxford University Press.
Grammar is a teacher resource book containing many practical activities, emphasizing student concordancing to find patterns for function vocabulary, genre analysis, dictation and drills. It has been a classroom staple for years.

Ur, P. (1988). *Grammar practice activities: A practical guide for teachers.* Cambridge: Cambridge University Press.
This book has been a major grammar activity book for years, although it lacks more recent corpus-based tasks. The book provides many useful grammar practice activities and explains how to use them in language classrooms. Many of the activities can be adapted for various communicative uses and form-focused activities.

Part II

Interaction- and Output-based Options in Focus on Grammar

Chapter 5

Focus on Grammar through Interactional Feedback

Introduction

In the previous chapter, we examined textual enhancement as a tool to focus on grammar in communicative context. This approach was concerned with raising learners' attention to grammatical forms by making target forms perceptually more salient through typographical manipulation of certain aspects of the input. In this chapter, we will discuss interactional feedback as another technique to draw learners' attention to grammatical forms in communicative contexts. This approach is based on an interactionist perspective to SLA and the assumption that negotiated interaction (i.e., interactional modifications made in the course of conversation) is essential for language acquisition. It has been proposed that, through negotiation, learners not only communicate their meaning, but can also receive corrective feedback on their ill-formed utterances through the use of conversational strategies such as clarification requests, confirmation checks, repetition, recasts, etc., that take place during interaction (e.g., Gass, 2003; Gass & Varonis, 1994; Long, 1991, 1996; Pica, 1994, 1998).

Theoretical Background

The extent to which language learners need corrective feedback in order to acquire language has been a matter of debate in L1 and L2 acquisition. Corrective feedback refers to utterances that indicate to the learner that his or her output is erroneous in some way (Lightbown & Spada, 1999). In the SLA literature, such feedback has also been called *negative evidence*, defined as information that tells the learner what is not possible in a given language, and has been contrasted with *positive evidence*, defined as information that tells the learner what is possible in a given language. Negative evidence is obtained in different ways such as through grammatical explanations or various forms of explicit and implicit corrective feedback on learners' non-targetlike utterances (Long, 1996). Positive evidence is received mainly through exposure to correct models of language in the input.

In the field of L1 acquisition, one theoretical position, known as the nativist theory, has claimed that there is a limited provision of explicit negative feedback in L1 learning (e.g., R. Brown & Hanlon, 1970; Demetras, Post, & Snow, 1986). Therefore, in order to learn language, children rely mainly on some innate principles, or what is called Universal Grammar (UG) (e.g., Chomsky, 1965). An alternative position, known as the interactionist perspective, postulates that negative feedback is not only available to children, but is also necessary for language acquisition. According to this position, when children interact with adults, they receive negative feedback through various forms of semantically contingent interactional adjustments made in response to their erroneous utterances (e.g., Farrar, 1990, 1992; Saxton, 1997). Although the degree to which children attend to this feedback or the mechanisms whereby it facilitates learning in L1 is still not clear, L1-based studies have provided strong evidence that negative feedback exists in child–parent interactions and that it contributes to L1 development (see Mitchell & Myles, 2004, for a review).

In the field of L2 acquisition, some researchers have argued that similar innate principles to those suggested to be available to L1 learners are also available fully or partially to L2 learners and that L2 learners do not need negative evidence, or if they do, it is only in rare cases where positive evidence is not enough to trigger the UG principles (e.g., Flynn, 1996; Schwartz, 1993). However, although such a perspective exists in the field of L2 acquisition, the majority of SLA researchers believe that L2 learning is different from child L1 learning, and that adult L2 learners cannot develop native-like accuracy simply on the basis of exposure to positive evidence or models of grammatical input (e.g., Carroll & Swain, 1993; DeKeyser, 1998; Doughty & Long, 2003; R. Ellis, 2001a; R. Ellis, Loewen, & Erlam, 2006; Mackey, Oliver, & Leeman, 2003; Pica, 2002). Therefore, L2 learners need both negative and positive feedback in order to acquire an L2 successfully.

Interactional Feedback

Many SLA researchers are currently examining the potential sources of negative feedback in L2 development. One line of such research, influenced by L1 child interaction research, has studied the nature of conversational interaction between native and non-native speakers (e.g., Doughty, 1994; Gass, Mackey, & Pica, 1998; Gass & Varonis, 1994; Long, 1983, 1996; Pica, 1994). This research has found that interactional feedback characteristic of L1 interaction also exists in L2 interaction. For example, it has found that when learners interact with a native speaker, they receive negative feedback through various forms of modification and negotiation strategies, such as clarification requests, repetitions, confirmation checks, etc., that occur in the course of interaction (e.g., Long, 1996, Gass, 2003; Gass & Varonis, 1994; Pica, 1994, 1988).

An important source of theoretical support for interactional feedback in L2 acquisitions is provided by Long's interaction hypothesis (Long 1996). This hypothesis claims that interaction has positive effects on L2 learning. These effects occur through a process called *negotiation*, defined as interactional modifications that occur "when learners and their interlocutors anticipate, perceive, or experience difficulties in message comprehensibility" (Pica, 1994, p. 494). Long proposed that negotiation for meaning is facilitative of L2 acquisition "because it connects input, internal learner capacities, particularly selective attention, and output in productive ways" (1996, pp. 451–52). Pica (1994) suggested that negotiation assists L2 development in three ways: by making message comprehensible, by enhancing L2 input, and by facilitating the production of modified output (learners' revisions of their erroneous output following feedback).

The argument for the role of interactional feedback is also closely connected with the importance attributed to FonF. As noted in Chapter 1, Long (1991) defined FonF as an approach in which attention to form occurs incidentally and in the context of communication and meaningful interaction. FonF occurs either reactively in response to learners' errors or proactively in a pre-planned manner. Interactional feedback constitutes a kind of reactive FonF as it occurs in reaction to learners' non-target-like utterances.

Different Types of Interactional Feedback

Interactional feedback can occur in different ways. In general, two broad categories of such feedback can be distinguished: reformulations and elicitations (Nassaji, 2007a). Reformulations are those feedback strategies that rephrase a learner's erroneous production, providing the learner with the correct form. Elicitations, on the other hand, do not provide learners with the correct form. Instead, they push or prompt the learner directly or indirectly to self-correct. These two feedback categories have also been called input providing and output prompting strategies (e.g., R. Ellis, 2009). Interactional feedback can be provided either extensively or intensively (R. Ellis, 2001a). Extensive feedback refers to feedback that is provided on a wide range of forms. Intensive feedback refers to feedback provided on certain preselected forms.

The aim of interactional feedback can either be conversational, in which the interlocutor attempts to deal with problems of message comprehensibly, or pedagogical when the interlocutor understands the message, but still attempts to correct the learner error or push the learner to produce a more formally correct or appropriate utterance. Conversational feedback involves *negotiation of meaning*, defined as side sequences to the flow of interaction "when a listener signals to a speaker that the speaker's message is not clear, and the listener and speaker both work linguistically to resolve the problem" (Pica, 1992, p. 200). Pedagogical feedback involves *negotiation of form*, defined as more deliberate attempts to draw learners' attention to form (Van den Branden, 1997).

In the following section, we will describe the different types and subtypes of interactional feedback along with examples. These strategies have been identified in a number of studies on how teachers react to learner errors during conversational interaction (e.g., R. Ellis, Basturkmen, & Loewen, 2001; Lyster, 1998; Lyster & Ranta, 1997; Panova & Lyster, 2002; Y. Sheen, 2004) and have been shown to facilitate L2 acquisition.

Recasts

One type of interactional feedback that has received much attention in the field of SLA is the recast. Recasts refer to utterances that reformulate the whole or part of the learner's erroneous utterance into a correct form while maintaining the overall focus on meaning (Nicholas, Lightbown, & Spada, 2001). The reformulation not only provides the learner with the correct form but may also signal to the learner that his or her utterance is deviant is some way. In other words, the feedback "draws learners' attention to mismatches between input and output," and hence "causes them to focus on form" (Long & Robinson, 1998, p. 25). Doughty and Varela (1998) described recasts as "potentially effective, since the aim is to add attention to form to a primarily communicative task rather than to depart from an already communicative goal in order to discuss a linguistic feature" (p. 114). The following provides an example of a recast.

Example (1)

STUDENT: And they found out the one woman run away.
TEACHER: OK, the woman was running away. [*Recast*]
STUDENT: Running away.

(Nassaji, 2009, p. 429)

In the above example, the recast has been triggered by the learner's utterance that contains an error related to the verb tense. The teacher has provided a recast by reformulating the learner's incorrect form into a correct form without changing the overall meaning. The learner has modified his original utterance by repeating the feedback.

In the SLA literature, the immediate response of the learner to the feedback has been called *uptake* (e.g., Lyster & Ranta, 1997). Uptake is an optional move in that learners may or may not respond to the feedback (R. Ellis et al., 2001). However, it has been used extensively in SLA research as a measure of feedback effectiveness. Chaudron (1977, p. 440), for example, pointed out that "the main immediate measurement of effectiveness of any type of corrective reaction would be a frequency count of the students' correct responses following each type." Uptake can be either successful when the learner correctly modifies his or her original utterance or unsuccessful when the learner does not correct his or her erroneous output (R. Ellis et al., 2001). Of course, although the learner may provide uptake in response to feedback, this does not indicate that the learner has acquired the form. It is possible that the learner is simply mimicking the teacher's feedback without much understanding (Gass, 2003). However, such learner responses have been considered to contribute to L2 acquisition because they may indicate that the learner has noticed the feedback and has made some use of it (Mackey & Philp, 1998).

Types of Recasts

Recasts are generally considered as implicit feedback because they imply rather than overtly correct the error. They are also unobtrusive because they rephrase an utterance without breaking the flow of communication. However, such interactional moves are complex, taking many different forms during interaction, differing from one another in terms of their degree of explicitness (Nassaji, 2007a, 2009). For example, recasts may occur in the form of declarative statements to confirm a learner's message (Lyster, 1998), in which case they can be considered fairly implicit, as in Example 2. In this example, the teacher provides a recast of the student's utterance but the feedback is implicit; thus, it can be ambiguous in that the student may either interpret the reformulation as corrective feedback or simply as confirming his or her statement. Recasts, however, can also occur in conjunction with additional intonational signals such as added stress, in which case they are more explicit (such as in Example 3). In such cases, the added stress may make the feedback more noticeable, drawing the learners' attention to the correct form more effectively.

Example (2)

TEACHER: OK. Everything was on sale. Why?
STUDENT: Because ... baseball winner.
TEACHER: OK. Because they won the Japan series. Do you like baseball?

(Nabei & Swain, 2002, p. 50)

Example (3)

STUDENT: And she catched her.
TEACHER: She CAUGHT [*added stress*] her?
STUDENT: Yeah, caught her.

(Nassaji, 2007b, p. 59)

The degree of explicitness of the recast may also vary depending on the number of changes it involves or the length of the feedback (see Philp, 2003). For example, a recast may reformulate part of the utterance or it may correct only one of the errors in a learner's utterance. Alternatively, it may correct multiple errors or even may expand on a learner's utterance by continuing the topic. A shorter recast involving only one correction is relatively more explicit than a longer recast that involves multiple corrections with topic continuation because the former can draw the learner's attention to form more directly than the latter (R. Ellis & Sheen, 2006; Loewen & Philp, 2006; Nassaji, 2007a). The following demonstrates an example of a recast correcting a single error and a recast correcting multiple errors with topic continuation.

Example (4)

STUDENT: The boy put the snake in the box and then ...
TEACHER: In a box? [*Single error corrected*]

(Y. Sheen, 2008, p. 850)

Example (5)

NNS: Ohh, she put on the apron?
NS: He put an apron on so he wouldn't get messy. [*Multiple errors corrected with topic continuation*]
NNS: Cooking?

(Braidi, 2002, p. 42)

Clarification Requests

Clarification requests occur when the teacher or an interlocutor does not fully understand a learner's utterance and then asks the learner to rephrase the utterance so that it can be clearer. The request may be motivated by either an error in the learner's utterance or it may be because the utterance is not comprehensible in some other way. The feedback does not provide the learner with the correct form. However, it may indicate to the learner that his or her utterance may contain an error. Since the feedback is interrogative, it provides the learner with an opportunity to self-repair. Clarification requests can be achieved by using phrases such as "pardon me?" or "sorry?" or "excuse me?" etc. The following provides an example of a clarification request.

Example (6)

STUDENT: I want practice today, today.
TEACHER: I'm sorry? [*Clarification request*]

(Panova & Lyster, 2002, p. 583)

Repetition

Interactional feedback can also occur in the form of repetition of all or part of the learner's erroneous utterances with a rising intonation. Like clarification requests, such feedback moves do not provide the learner with the correct form. However, they may indicate that the learner's utterance is erroneous, thus, providing the learner with an opportunity to self-repair. The following provides an example of repetition.

Example (7)

STUDENT: Oh my God, it is too expensive, I pay only 10 dollars.
TEACHER: I pay? [*Repetition with rising intonation*]
STUDENT 2: Okay let's go.

(Y. Sheen, 2004, p. 279)

Metalinguistic Feedback

Metalinguistic feedback refers to feedback that provides the learner with metalinguistic comments (i.e., comments about language) in the form of a statement or a question about the correctness of an utterance. This feedback may either simply involve metalinguistic hints or clues about the location or the nature of the error (e.g., "Can you correct the verb?" or "You need an adverb.") or it may include metalinguistic explanation in conjunction with correction. The following provides examples of a metalinguistic clue and metalinguistic feedback with correction.

Example (8)

STUDENT: I see him in the office yesterday.
TEACHER: You need a past tense. [*Metalinguistic clue*]

Example (9)

STUDENT: He catch the fish.
TEACHER: Caught is the past tense. [*Metalinguistic feedback with correction*]

Direct Elicitation

Direct elicitation refers to feedback strategies that attempt more overtly to elicit the correct form from the learner. This may take the form of repeating the learner's utterance up to the point where the error has occurred and waiting for the learner to complete the utterance such as "He went ... ?" Or it may take the form of a query that asks the learner more directly to repeat his or her utterance such as "Can you repeat what you said?" None of these strategies involves correction, but they may indicate indirectly to the learner that there is something wrong with their utterance. Thus, the feedback may draw the learners' attention to the problematic form and push the learner to self-correct. The following from Nassaji (2007a) shows examples of such elicitation strategies.

Example (10)

STUDENT: And when the young girl arrive, ah, beside the old woman.
TEACHER: When the young girl ... ?

(p. 529)

Example (11)

STUDENT: She easily catched the girl.
TEACHER: She catched the girl? I'm sorry, say that again.

(p. 528)

Direct Correction

Direct correction refers to feedback that identifies the error and then overtly corrects it. This type of feedback has the advantage of providing the learner with clear information about how to correct the error. However, since the feedback supplies the correction, it does not provide the learner with an opportunity to self-repair. Thus, the feedback may not result in any negotiation or learners' active participation in the feedback process (Lyster, 1998; Lyster & Ranta, 1997). The following provides an example of a direct correction.

Example (12)

STUDENT: He has catch a cold.
TEACHER: Not catch, caught. [*Direct correction*]
STUDENT: Oh, ok.

Nonverbal Feedback

Feedback can also be provided nonverbally using body movements and signals such as gestures, facial expressions, head, hand, and finger movements. For example, shaking the head or frowning could be used to indicate the presence of an error. Arms, hand, or figure movements could be used to indicate the nature of the error.

Example (13)

STUDENT: My mom cooks always good food.
TEACHER: [Crosses over arms in front of the body to indicate word order]

When using nonverbal feedback, it might be useful if the teacher familiarizes students in advance with the kinds of body movements he or she might use. For example, the teacher may inform students that when he or she crosses over his or her arms in front of the boy, it indicates a problem with word order.

Interactional Feedback on Written Errors

The bulk of the literature on interactional feedback has been on oral errors. However, such feedback can also be used to address written errors. When students make errors in their written work, teachers can address these errors through interactional negotiations conducted after the task is completed in the same or subsequent sessions. Examples of such feedback can be seen in

Nassaji (2007c), which documented the occurrence of such feedback in an adult ESL classroom. In the classes observed, students wrote weekly journals on topics that they liked. The teacher reviewed the journals, identified samples of erroneous utterances that included common errors, and then conducted follow-up oral feedback sessions in response to those utterances in the next class. The teacher used various forms of feedback including reformulations and elicitations. He also varied his strategies depending on the nature of the error, thus providing feedback exchanges that differed from one another in terms of the amount of negotiation, ranging from feedback with limited negotiation to feedback with extended negotiation. The following illustrates examples of feedback exchanges with limited and extended negotiations.

Example (14): limited negotiation

STUDENT: It's cheaper than Canadian's one. [*Erroneous utterance*]
TEACHER: It's cheaper than Canadian's one?
STUDENT: Canadians.
TEACHER: The Canadian. The s is in the wrong place. A pack of cigarettes is cheaper than Canadian ones.

(Nassaji, 2007c, p. 124)

The above example displays a feedback exchange with two feedback moves. The feedback is triggered in response to the problematic use of the word "Canadian." The teacher has initially used an elicitation strategy to push the learner to correct the form. The learner responds to the teacher's elicitation but her response fails to correct the error. Following the student's unsuccessful response, the teacher provides the correct answer by using a direct correction along with a metalinguistic explanation, alerting the learner that the "s" has been used wrongly.

The following shows an example of a feedback exchange involving more negotiation.

Example (15): extended negotiation

STUDENT: Teachers in class like our friend ... [*Erroneous utterance*]
TEACHER: So who can make a correction? Who's got an idea to correct this? Mitny what would you do to correct this? Any idea?
STUDENT: I don't know. I don't know.
TEACHER: Just try. Just try. Just try your best.
STUDENT: Okay, okay. Their.
TEACHER: OK so there is "their"?
STUDENT: Their teachers?
TEACHER: How about I'll help here. How about "our teachers"?
STUDENT: Our teachers?
TEACHER: Can you start with that?
STUDENT: Our teachers?

TEACHER: Yeah.

STUDENT: Hm. Hm. They are?

TEACHER: OK. So we have "teachers," so we don't need "their." We just need "teachers are."

(Nassaji, 2007c, p. 124)

In the above example, the feedback is triggered by a problem in the use of the plural verb "are." The teacher begins the feedback by redirecting the correction to students, asking if anyone knows how to make a correction. The teacher then asks the student, who responds that she does not know the correct form. Upon the learner's initial failure, the teacher pushes the learner further in her output, providing the learner with extra opportunities to self-correct. The teacher has tried to adjust the feedback to the learner's need by moving from using indirect feedback to more direct feedback, helping the learner gradually towards correction. The type of feedback seen in this exchange is in line with the idea of scaffolding as put forward by Vygotsky (see Chapter 7) and the idea of feedback within the learner's zone of proximal development (ZPD) (Aljaafreh & Lantolf, 1994; Nassaji & Swain, 2000).

Which Errors Should be Corrected?

A fundamental question in error correction asks what kinds of errors should be corrected (Hendrickson, 1978). The distinction between *errors* and *mistakes* (Corder, 1967) or *local* and *global* errors (Burt & Kiparsky, 1974) might be helpful when making decisions about what errors should be corrected (R. Ellis, 2009). *Errors* occur because of a lack of knowledge but *mistakes* are simply performance errors. *Local errors* do not affect general understanding of the message and usually have to do with minor errors such as those related to the omission of morphological markers or function words. *Global errors*, however, cause problems in communication and include errors such as wrong word order or inappropriate uses of lexical items. Teachers may be advised to pay more attention to errors than mistakes and to global errors rather than local errors. Hendrickson (1978) also recommended that teachers might prioritize errors based on their frequency of occurrence or the stigmatizing effects they may have on the interlocutor (that is the unfavorable reaction the error elicits towards the learner). Of course, such recommendations may not be easy in practice, as it is not always easy to distinguish errors from mistakes (R. Ellis, 2009). For example, if errors occur during a grammatical exercise, it is possible that the cause is incomplete knowledge of the grammar, but if they occur during a communicative activity, it is hard to know what the exact cause is (Chastain, 1981).

Empirical Research on Interactional Feedback

A substantial body of empirical research has recently examined the occurrence and effectiveness of different types of interactional feedback. Studies have been conducted both inside and outside the classroom (e.g., in laboratory settings) and have also used various measures to assess effectiveness, ranging from learners' uptake to various forms of pre- and post-test measures. In this section, we will briefly review a selected sample of such studies (see articles in Mackey, 2007; and Mackey & Gass, 2006 for a more comprehensive review).

One of the studies of interactional feedback is by Lyster and Ranta (1997), which investigated the occurrence and effectiveness of interactional feedback in content-based French immersion classrooms. This research showed that recasts occurred most frequently in such classrooms, but they generated the least amount of uptake in comparison to other feedback types such as clarification requests, elicitations, and metalinguistic feedback. Panova and Lyster (2002) examined the occurrence of feedback in an adult ESL classroom. The study replicated Lyster and Ranta's (1997) results, finding that recasts were used frequently, but led to limited degree of learner uptake. R. Ellis et al. (2001) examined the use of interactional feedback in an adult ESL context in New Zealand. They found very frequent use of recasts; however, unlike Lyster and Ranta's study, they found a high degree of successful uptake following recasts. The researchers attributed this difference to the difference in the context of study (i.e., content-based French immersion vs. adult intensive ESL programs) (see also Y. Sheen, 2004). Doughty and Varela (1998) investigated the effectiveness of recasts in a classroom experimental study. Recasts were used in the form of reformulation of the error along with added stress and repetition. The study found that the group who received such recasts outperformed in both accuracy and use of the targeted form (English past tense) those who did not receive them. In another experimental study, Lyster (2004) compared the effects of recasts and elicitation strategies (what they called prompts) on learning French grammatical gender, when used in conjunction with form-focused instruction. They found that the group who received elicitations outperformed the ones receiving recasts. This study suggests that elicitation strategies are more effective than recasts when combined with explicit instruction (see also Ammar & Spada, 2006).

There are also a number of studies that have examined the effectiveness of interactional feedback outside classroom contexts. Mackey and Philp (1998) examined the effects of recasts on L2 learner's development of question formation, and found that learners (particularly advanced learners) who received recasts benefited more from the feedback than those who did not receive recasts. Philp (2003) examined learners' noticing of recasts in dyadic task-based interaction. The results showed that learners were able to notice a substantial amount of the recasts (60–70%), although the results also varied depending on the learners' language level and length of recasts. Nassaji (2007a, 2009) examined the effectiveness of recasts versus elicitations in dyadic interactions, and found that explicit forms of recasts were more effective than implicit forms of recasts and elicitations. Loewen and Nabei (2007) examined the effects of three feedback types on question formation in

English: recasts, clarification requests, and metalinguistic feedback. The study found that the groups that received feedback performed better than the group that received no feedback on timed grammaticality judgment tests. No difference was found across feedback types.

Studies that have examined the effectiveness of interactional feedback have found that in general such feedback is beneficial for L2 learning. However, they have also found that the effectiveness of interactional feedback depends on a variety of factors, including the nature of the feedback, the type of linguistic form focused on as well as the context in which the feedback is provided.

Suggestions for Teachers

Based on the literature on interactional feedback and studies that have examined its effectiveness, the following recommendations can be made:

1 For interactional feedback to be effective, learners must notice the corrective force of the feedback. Therefore, teachers should make sure that the feedback is salient enough to be noticed.
2 Feedback may be more effective when targeting a single linguistic feature at a time rather than a wide range of forms. Thus, teachers should select specific types of errors and target them in each lesson (R. Ellis, 2009).
3 Recasts are potentially ambiguous, as learners may perceive them as feedback on content rather than on form. Recasts may become more effective if disambiguated with additional, more explicit, verbal and phonological prompts (i.e., added stress, repetition, etc.).
4 Elicitations may be more effective than reformulations as these feedback strategies push learners to self-correct, and therefore, engage learners more actively in the feedback process than reformulations (Lyster, 2004). Therefore, when providing feedback, it might be advisable to begin with an elicitation. But if the strategy fails to lead to self-correction, recasts can then be provided.
5 Elicitations lead to self-correction only if learners already have some knowledge of the targeted form. Therefore, elicitations may be more effective for more advanced learners who are able to recognize and correct their errors than beginner learners who are not able to do so. If the learner does not know the target form and the teacher still pushes the learner to self-correct, this might embarrass the learner as it may publicly reveal his or her lack of knowledge (Long, 2006).
6 Learners learn best when they are developmentally ready. Thus, the teacher should attempt to adjust the feedback to the learners' developmental level. This suggestion, however, may not easily work in practice as it is difficult to determine whether a particular learner is developmentally ready to process a particular feedback type (R. Ellis, 2005). One helpful strategy, however, would be using negotiated feedback, that is, feedback that begins

with indirect hints and then gradually and progressively moves towards more direct help based on the learner's need and responses. An example of this was seen above (Example 15). Another example can be seen in the following feedback exchange between a tutor and a learner from Nassaji and Swain (2000, pp. 41–42).

TEACHER: "I think I am such stupid girl." There is something wrong with this sentence. Can you see?
STUDENT: Such stupid the girl?
TEACHER: No.
STUDENT: No?
TEACHER: There is something wrong with "stupid."
STUDENT: Uh … stupidary?
TEACHER: I mean there is something wrong with "stupid girl."
STUDENT: Article? Need article?
TEACHER: Yes.
STUDENT: But … but …
TEACHER: Which … what article?
STUDENT: Ah … a?

7 Feedback that encourages uptake is more effective than feedback without uptake (recall that uptake refers to learners' immediate response following feedback). Thus, teachers should use more feedback moves that provide opportunities for uptake and modified output (such as elicitations or recasts in conjunction with prompts to push the learner to respond to feedback).

8 The effectiveness of feedback depends on the social and instructional context in which the feedback occurs. Therefore, teachers should be aware of the differences in classroom contexts and adjust the feedback strategies they use to suit the situations in which they teach (see also Chapter 8).

9 Learners are different and learn in different ways. Thus, teachers should be aware of individual learner differences (see, for example, Dornyei, 2006; Dornyei & Skehan, 2003) and use their feedback strategies accordingly.

10 No matter what kind of strategies teachers use, they should be careful not to overuse corrective feedback, as excessive corrective feedback can have negative consequences leading to learners' disappointment and discouragement.

Classroom Activities

Basically, teachers can provide interactional feedback on learners' utterances during any classroom activity that involves learners speaking with the teacher or other students. What needs to be done is to create opportunities for such interactions. One way of achieving this would be through using various kinds of interactive group work activities as well as class discussions and presentations. A few examples of such activities are presented below.

Activity 1. Interactional Feedback during Group Work Activities

The following from Hawkes (2007) shows an example of a small group work activity involving feedback that can also be used in the classroom.

Situation: Students are told that their school needs to hire a new English teacher and that, as a group, the students need to decide which of the applicants to hire.

1 Students are divided into groups of three or four. Each student is given a different (fictional) CV and is required to share the information on the CV with the other students.
2 Students discuss and come to a consensus on which applicant is the best person to be hired.
3 The teacher goes around the class and provides interactional feedback on erroneous utterances.

Activity 2. Interactional Feedback during Class Discussions, Presentations, and Student-Teacher Interactions

Interactional feedback can also be provided during different kinds of class discussions, presentations, and other occasions when students and teacher have interactions. There are many ways to promote classroom discussions such as introducing a topic related to a classroom activity (e.g., a reading, listening or even writing activity) or other topics that may be of interest, and asking students to express their opinions about that topic (see Lazaraton, 2001, for a discussion of various kinds of dicsussion activities that can be implemented in the classroom). As an example, the teacher may ask the class to discuss the role of computer in language learning or express their opinions about advantages and disadvantages of living in a big city, etc. If students make erroneous statements while discussing the issue, the teacher can draw their attention to the error by using interactional feedback (e.g., recasts, repetitions, clarification requests, metalinguistic feedback, etc.).

Activity 3. Feedback on Students' Questions using Tic Tac Toe

The above examples show activities that provide opportunities for open discussion, and also feedback on any error that learners make in the course of interaction. Teachers can also use more structured classroom tasks that elicit certain target structures and then provide feedback on those structures (see Chapter 6 for discussion and examples of such tasks). The following activity from Bell (2008) illustrates an example of such a task in an ESL classroom. The target structure is ESL question formation and the elicitation task is a tic tac toe game. This is a game consisting of a blank grid that two players fill in with Xs and Os to make complete rows in vertical, horizontal and diagonal directions. The game is considered over when no squares in the grid remain and the player with the highest number of completed rows wins the game.

1 Students are presented with a game board that contains nine vocabulary cards in three rows of three. The cards are placed face down so that students do not see what the card shows. There is one vocabulary word or phrase on each card that is familiar to the student.

2 Students are divided into teams: A and B. Students from each team come to the front of the class to play the game. They take turns selecting one of the cards from the grid and make a question with the word on the card.

3 When students make the question with an error, the teacher provides recasts in response to the erroneous utterances (please note that the use of tic tac toe is simply to elicit questions). The teacher can provide any other type of feedback. The game can be adapted so that teams of students can play at once.

Conclusion

In this chapter, we discussed interactional feedback as one way of drawing learners' attention to grammatical forms in the course of communicative interaction. We presented the different types of feedback along with examples and also discussed what SLA theory and research suggest about their effectiveness. The teaching implications of the findings of interactional feedback research were discussed. However, we should keep in mind that language learning is a complex and gradual process and that we should not expect that a reaction in response to learner errors in the course of interaction would necessarily lead to immediate substantial effects. Interactional feedback might work best when combined with other types of form-focused activities including explicit instruction (see Lyster, 2004).

Questions for Reflection

1 How do you treat spoken errors in your classroom? What corrective technique do you use most often, and why? Among error types (e.g., grammatical, lexical, pronunciation), do you have any preference for correcting one type of error more often than others?

2 Interactional feedback is often immediate as it occurs in response to an error at the time it is committed. However, students may also receive feedback on their errors with some delay, after they have completed the classroom task. Which of the two feedback types do you think is more effective: immediate or delayed, and why?

3 As we noted above, a number of recommendations have been made in the literature about what kind of error should be corrected (e.g., errors can be selected based on their frequency of occurrence, their stigmatizing effects, or the degree to which they hinder communication). How feasible do you think these recommendations are? As a teacher, how would you choose whether or not an error should be corrected?

4 Oral corrective feedback is a viable strategy only if students participate in communicative interaction. If you have a student who does not participate in classroom interaction or discussions, what approach would you take in order to improve his or her participation?

5 Being publicly corrected in front of others can be a stressful situation for learners. As a teacher, how would you overcome this problem, knowing that some errors need to be more overtly corrected than others?

Useful Resources

Hendrickson, J. (1978). "Error correction in foreign language teaching: Recent theory, research, and practice." *Modern Language Journal, 62,* 387–98.

This classic article on error correction gives insight into the history of error correction in second language teaching. It illustrates how L2 teaching has gradually moved away from an error prevention methodology to the contemporary approach of embracing errors and using them for learning experiences in a communicative setting. It discusses a number of fundamental questions about corrective feedback such as whether or not errors should be corrected, when they should be corrected, and which errors should be corrected.

Long, M. (2000). "Focus on form in task-based language teaching." In R. D. Lambert & E. Shohamy (Eds.), *Language policy and pedagogy: Essays in honor of Ronald Walton* (pp. 179–92). Philadelphia, PA: John Benjamins.

This article seeks to explain the superiority of a focus on form approach compared with teaching linguistic forms in isolation. It explains how addressing linguistic-code features as they arise in communicative context can assist language acquisition. This is useful for teachers who are looking at ways to incorporate attention to form into a task-based methodology.

Lyster, R., & Ranta, L. (1997). "Corrective feedback and learner uptake: Negotiation of form in communicative classrooms." *Studies in Second Language Acquisition, 19,* 37–66.

This paper explains an extensive study done on corrective feedback and learners' reaction to it in French immersion classrooms. It describes each of the corrective feedback types used in the classrooms along with examples (i.e., recasts, elicitations, explicit correction, repetition, and metalinguistic feedback). This article is helpful in demonstrating what sorts of corrective feedback teachers use in content-based classrooms and which is most effective in resulting in learner uptake.

Mackey, A. (Ed.) (2007). *Conversational interaction in second language acquisition: A collection of empirical studies.* Oxford: Oxford University Press.

This volume brings together a number of recent empirical studies that have investigated the role of interaction and feedback in L2 learning. In the Introduction, the editor provides a useful discussion of a number of issues related to interactional processes and how they assist L2 acquisition, such as noticing, the production of modified output, and the relationship between interactional feedback and learning. Each of the studies included examines aspects of these processes.

Pica, T. (1994). "Research on negotiation: What does it reveal about second-language learning conditions, processes, and outcomes?" *Language Learning,* *44*, 493–527.

This article looks at negotiation as a facilitator of L2 development in communicative settings. It discusses how negotiation can be a method of feedback for L2 learners, and examines how their output is modified based on this feedback. It also provides a useful review of research showing how negotiation is useful and how it can have positive effects on L2 learning.

Chapter 6

Focus on Grammar through Structured Grammar-Focused Tasks

Introduction

This chapter takes a task-based approach to teaching grammar in communicative contexts. However, it is not about tasks in general, as that subject has been the topic of numerous books and articles (e.g., R. Ellis, 2003; Nunan, 2004; Robinson & Gilabert, 2007; Samuda & Bygate, 2008), and specific tasks are discussed in other chapters (Chapters 3 and 7). In this chapter we are dealing with a special type of task which has the target grammar point presented implicitly or explicitly as the task content. These are structured grammar-focused tasks, also called grammar consciousness-raising tasks.

Background and Rationale

As we have emphasized, it is now widely acknowledged that formal instruction on grammar forms is necessary to promote L2 learner accuracy and high levels of target language attainment (e.g., Doughty & Long, 2003; R. Ellis, 1982, 1994, 1997; Robinson, 2001; Williams, 2005). As mentioned, the main reason for the failure of the communicative approaches that dominated pedagogy in much of North America during the 1970s and 1980s was evidence from communicatively-based immersion programs with various target languages indicating the learners continued to make output errors despite years of study. Thus, it is now recognized that it is essential to make the target language structure obvious to the learner, whether through formal instruction or through manipulation of communicative input, in ways that call attention to target forms and allow learners to process them, or a combination of these methods. As we have noted, input, output, and feedback on output are seen as essential for L2 acquisition, and research suggests that learner uptake is especially successful when negotiated interaction occurs, when form-focused activities are complex rather than simple, and when interaction is student-initiated (R. Ellis, 2003; Nassaji & Fotos, 2004; Samuda & Bygate 2008). One way to meet these requirements is through performing tasks.

Many definitions of tasks have been proposed. Nunan (1989) defined a task as "a piece of classroom work which involves learners in comprehending, manipulating, producing or interacting in the target language while their attention is principally focused on meaning rather than form" (p. 10). R. Ellis (2003, p. 16) defined tasks as "a work plan that requires learners to process language pragmatically in order to achieve an outcome that can be evaluated in terms of whether the correct or appropriate propositional content has been conveyed." Willis and Willis (2007) defined tasks as activities "where the target language is used by the learner for a communicative purpose (goal) in order to achieve an outcome" (p. 173). Skehan (1996b, p. 20) defined tasks as "activities which have meaning as their primary focus" and "generally bear some resemblance to real-life language use." Thus, according to these definitions, the primary focus of tasks is on meaning rather than form.

Tasks are not only considered to be instructional activities in the classroom but also as units for planning and organizing the curriculum or syllabus (R. Ellis, 2003; Nunan, 2004; Samuda & Bygate, 2008), especially by encouraging learner empowerment and individualized learning. A distinction has been made between convergent tasks, where learners agree on a task solution through information exchange (e.g., Samuda & Bygate, 2008; Skehan, 1996a) and divergent tasks, where learners take a stand on an issue and present their argument. This particular task type leads to syntactic complexity and longer turns, more output and, thus, more comprehensible input for the listener.

Task-based instruction has been shown to promote the type of negotiated interaction that leads to noticing and awareness (see Bygate, Skehan, & Swain, 2001; R. Ellis, 2003) and provides quality input (Lightbown, 1992), defined as input rich in communicative usages of problematic target structures. Research has demonstrated that it is through the provision of both comprehensible input (Gass et al., 1998; Pica, 1991, 1996, 2002) and the need to produce output (Swain, 1993; Swain & Lapkin, 1995) that language acquisition is suggested to take place. Thus, in task-based instruction, the acquisition of the target structures is promoted through opportunities to hear meaningful input, to produce the target language in response to the input, and to receive feedback on learner production.

Task-based instruction has been traditionally based on the idea that if learners are to learn the target language successfully, they must engage in activities that provide opportunities for naturalistic or real-life language use rather than activities that focus only on language forms (R. Ellis, 2003; Nunan, 2004; Samuda & Bygate, 2008). In other words, the focus must be on communicating a message rather than on a particular form (R. Ellis, 1982). However, this approach to task-based instruction has been found inadequate in promoting acceptable levels of accuracy in L2 learning (see Widdowson, 2003). Furthermore, a purely meaning-focused approach to task-based instruction is often problematic in the foreign language situation, where real-life needs for the target language rarely exist and learners are studying the target language mainly to pass written examinations (e.g., the considerations raised by Nassaji & Fotos, 2004).

Addressing these problems in a book on task-based instruction, R. Ellis (2003) made a distinction between focused and unfocused communicative tasks. Unfocused tasks deal with meaning, and are not intended to elicit target structures. Focused tasks, however, are designed to have a particular linguistic focus. They are aimed at making grammar forms salient to learners by using the forms in such a way that learners' attention is drawn to their use in context. Other researchers have also stressed the need to include a FonF component in task-based instruction, with some suggesting that the FonF should come at the end of the task-based cycle (Willis & Willis, 2007).

Structure-Based Focused Tasks

Researchers and teachers have increasingly advocated approaches to foreign language instruction that are task-based (Crookes & Gass, 1993a, 1993b; R. Ellis, 2003; Nunan, 1989, 2004; Samuda & Bygate, 2008). Some have recommended the use of tasks for accuracy practice (i.e., Ur, 1988), whereas others have emphasized their consciousness-raising function (Bygate et al., 2001; Dickins & Woods, 1988; García Mayo, 2007; Rutherford & Sharwood Smith, 1985). Recently structure-based focused tasks have been proposed that aim at making grammar forms obvious to the learner through consciousness-raising activities (R. Ellis, 2003; Nassaji & Fotos, 2004). Although learners' attention is drawn to the nature of the target structure, the tasks are communicative, since learners are engaged in meaning-focused interaction.

R. Ellis (2003) identified three types of structure-based focused tasks: (1) structure-based production tasks; (2) comprehension (interpretation) tasks; and (3) consciousness-raising tasks. Structure-based production tasks require the use of the target form to complete a communicative activity (Loschky & Bley-Vroman, 1993; Nassaji, 1999). This category may also include grammar tasks that require learners to practice certain target structures through various forms of production exercises. Comprehension tasks are designed so that learners must notice then process the target form in carefully designed input, usually a stimulus that requires a learner response containing the target item. According to R. Ellis (1995, p. 94), such tasks have the following goals:

1   To enable learners to identify the meaning(s) realized by a specific grammatical feature (i.e., to help them carry out a form-function mapping). In this case, the goal is grammar comprehension, to be distinguished from what might be termed message comprehension, which can take place without the learner having to attend to the grammatical form. For example, on hearing the sentence, "I'd like three bottles please," a learner may be able to understand that bottles is plural in meaning without noticing the s-morpheme or understanding its function.
2   To enhance input (Sharwood Smith, 1993) in such a way that learners are induced to notice a grammatical feature that they otherwise might ignore. In other words, interpretation tasks are designed to facilitate noticing.

3 To enable learners to carry out the kind of cognitive comparison that has been hypothesized to be important for interlanguage development. Learners need to be encouraged to notice the gap between the way a particular form works to convey meaning in the input and how they are using the same form or, alternatively, how they convey the meaning realized by the form when they communicate. One way of fostering this is to draw learners' attention to the kinds of errors that they typically make.

The third type, grammar consciousness-raising tasks, requires learners to communicate directly about grammar structures, perhaps by generating a rule for their use. These tasks may present the structure implicitly, embedded in communicative contexts or present the grammar structure explicitly as task content. R. Ellis (1993b) made a distinction between grammar consciousness-raising tasks and *practice* tasks. In the latter, learners practice the use of grammatical structures through production activities. The former involves "activities that will seek to get a learner to understand a particular grammatical feature, how it works, what it consists of, and so on, but not require that learner to actually produce sentences manifesting that particular structure" (pp. 6–7). This particular use of the term "consciousness raising" emphasizes the fact that it leads to noticing. Once noticing has occurred, task performance can be followed by other communicative activities containing the target structure to further enhance noticing. R. Ellis (2002) discusses the general concept of consciousness raising as follows: "Consciousness-raising ... involves an attempt to equip the learner with an understanding of a specific grammatical feature - to develop declarative rather than procedural knowledge of it" (p. 167).

The main characteristics of consciousness-raising activities, according to Ellis, are the following:

1 There is an attempt to *isolate* a specific linguistic feature for focused attention.
2 The learners are provided with *data* which illustrate the targeted feature and they may also be supplied with an *explicit rule* describing or explaining the feature.
3 The learners are expected to utilize *intellectual effort* to understand the targeted feature.
4 Misunderstanding or incomplete understanding of the grammatical structure by the learners leads to *clarification* in the form of further data and description or explanation.
5 Learners may be required (although this is not obligatory) to articulate the rule describing the grammatical structure (R. Ellis, 2002, p. 168).

Tasks based on grammar structures as content have repeatedly been found to be effective in promoting both negotiation of meaning and awareness of the target structure (see the review in Nassaji & Fotos, 2007; Robinson 2001).

Research on the use of such tasks has suggested that their effectiveness depends on the nature of the form used. For example, it has been found that structures which have few rules governing their use are better for focused task performance than structures with a great many rules (Samuda & Bygate, 2008; R. Ellis, 1995, 2003; DeKeyser, 1998; Robinson 1996). It has also been found (R. Ellis, 2003; Loschky & Bley-Vroman, 1993; Robinson 1996) that focused tasks containing communicative instances of the target form are useful for developing learner awareness of grammar structures which are too complex to be understood through formal instruction alone.

Grammar task research has provided a variety of formats to integrate grammar instruction and task-based instruction, giving methods to combine form-focused and meaning-focused activities that would suit various pedagogical positions, instructional styles or teaching situations. Nassaji (1999) made a distinction between the ways that a focus on form can be achieved in communicative tasks: through *design* and through *process*. The *design* method involves constructing tasks that have a deliberate focus on form component. In such tasks, "the teacher decides in advance what forms should be focused on" and then designs the task accordingly (Nassaji, 1999, p. 392). In the *process* method, the form comes to the attention of the learner as a result of completing the task. In the latter type, learners may attend to different forms, depending on their previous knowledge and specific task requirements. An example of process method tasks would be a spot-the-difference task, in which pairs of students communicate to find differences in two sets of pictures. As a result of completing this task, the learners' attention may be drawn to the accurate use of certain forms (e.g., locative prepositions) needed to express their meaning adequately. In such tasks, learners must not only use certain forms to complete the task but also must understand and process the form as used by the other learner. Thus, such tasks require both production and comprehension of certain forms to complete the communicative activity (Loschky & Bley-Vroman, 1993; see also articles in García Mayo, 2007).

In focused tasks, once learners become conscious of a grammar point, they often tend to notice it in subsequent communicative input. Such noticing appears to initiate the restructuring of the implicit system of linguistic knowledge. When a language point is noticed frequently, learners unconsciously compare the new input with their existing L2 system, construct new hypotheses and test them by attending to further input and by getting feedback on their own output using the new form. In this way, acquisition has occurred, and noticing has been a trigger. A few years ago, Fotos (1993, 1994) did a study of noticing, using learners who either performed grammar tasks or received grammar lessons. These learners significantly noticed the target structures in communicative input one and two weeks later, compared with a control group, who received no grammar instruction and did not perform grammar-based tasks. There were also indications that high levels of noticing were related to proficiency.

Grammar instruction can take different forms, varying in the degree of attention they require students to pay to the targeted structures. Thus, different options exist for consciousness-raising tasks that differ in the degree of explicitness. The following section describes implicit and explicit structured grammar-focused tasks that have been successfully used with ESL/EFL learners to provide opportunities for meaning-focused language use during activities that promote awareness of problematic grammatical structures.

Implicit Grammar-Focused Tasks

As noted, tasks are considered consciousness-raising if they are designed so that learners must notice and process the target form as they communicate their meaning. The fact that learners have to produce the form is important, both in terms of auto-input and in terms of receiving feedback from other learners. Those tasks which have an information gap and the need for a single, agreed-upon solution (Fotos, 1994) tend to produce the most task talk, and the increased output leads to a greater frequency of use of the target structure, which enhances noticing. Such tasks are easy to construct, with the option of giving the learners pre- and post tests to assess grammar gains.

Implicit structured grammar-focused tasks lend themselves to a variety of grammar structures and task contents. For example, as described above, a grammar task with an implicit focus on the target grammar structure is a drawing activity targeting locative prepositions. Without showing their partners, the learners draw a picture of different shapes inside a picture frame. When they are done, they give their partners instruction on how to draw the same picture. Then they compare their pictures. This task was used in EFL classrooms and produced gains in learner accuracy on the grammar point built into the task (Fotos, 1993). Another task was developed (Fotos, Homan, & Poel, 1994) on comparative forms of English adjectives and adverbs. Groups of three or four EFL learners were requested to present the features of cities they knew well to the other members of their group. The learners were then requested to combine their information by writing a number of English sentences comparing two cities. Although there was no mention of the target form, the learners had to understand and produce various comparative forms in order to complete the task. The requirement for the learners to produce sentences ensured that most of the interaction was conducted in the target language despite the homogenous L1 setting. The stories were presented to the rest of the class as comprehension exercises. The teacher then commented on the use of L1 comparative forms via a grammatical mini-lesson.

Implicit structured grammar-focused tasks have sometimes been used in conjunction with formal instruction before and summative activities after task performance. Research on explicit structured grammar-focused tasks

(R. Ellis, 2003; Fotos, 1993) suggests that not only can such tasks increase learner awareness of the target structure but they can also release more traditionally oriented non-native speakers (NNS) teachers in the EFL context from the requirement to lead communicative activities in the target language.

Explicit Grammar-Focused Tasks

This task type was developed for the EFL context (see Chapter 8) although it can be used effectively in ESL classrooms as well (Fotos, 1993, 1994; Fotos & Ellis, 1991; Nassaji & Fotos, 2004; Wong, 2005). It is also communicative, involving meaningful language exchange taking place as a primary task component, yet there is an explicit focus on form since the task content is the grammar structure itself. Learners are required to solve grammar problems through meaning-focused interaction and are often given task cards with sentences using the target structure to read to their group. It is often an information-gap task format, where learners have to listen to their task members presenting information that they do not have and take careful note of the information given. Based on combining the sentences presented by each group member and examining all of them, the group then constructs a rule for the use of the structure. The explicit grammar-structured grammar-focused task does not necessarily require immediate production of the grammar structure to complete the task solution, but rather attempts to call learners' attention to grammatical features and raise their awareness of them (R. Ellis, 2002). As R. Ellis, (1993a, p. 72) noted, "These are tasks designed to make the learners think about a particular grammatical feature in order to develop some degree of cognitive understanding." They can be designed in the form of deductive tasks, "where the learners are given a rule which they then apply (and possibly amend) to data provided." Or they can be inductive, "where they [learners] discover the rule for themselves by analysing the data provided." Thus, explicit structured grammar-focused task performance is suggested to have the potential to raise learners' consciousness of problematic grammar points so that they remain aware of them, and to push learners to make adjustments in their own output so that their use of the target form is more accurate.

Research on such tasks suggests (Fotos, 1993; Nassaji, 1999; Wong, 2005) that explicit structured grammar-focused tasks in communicative classrooms are as effective at promoting gains in explicit knowledge of the grammar feature as traditional grammar lessons, while maintaining the benefits of task performance. In addition, performance of the task produces amounts of L2 task talk comparable to talk produced by performance of meaning-focused communicative tasks. Additional research (Fotos, 1993, 1994; Nassaji, 2009; Nassaji & Fotos, 2004; Wong, 2005) also suggests that once learner awareness has been raised, learners are able to notice the structures in meaning-focused activities several weeks later.

The Selection of Target Forms for Structured Grammar-Focused Tasks

An important decision in constructing structured grammar-focused tasks is what form should be the focus of the task. One issue that complicates the matter is that forms differ from one another in terms of the degree to which they respond to form-focused instruction (Nassaji, 1999). However, R. Ellis (1995) has suggested two factors that are important to consider when selecting target structures for structured grammar-focused tasks: *problematicity* and *learnability*. *Problematicity* concerns the nature of the problem that the learner has with a particular target structure. Here the form can be determined based on systematic examination of samples of learners' production (R. Ellis, 1995) or they can be selected intuitively based on teachers' overall perception of learners' interlanguage needs (Nassaji, 1999). *Learnability* is the extent to which learners are able to integrate the target structure into their linguistic system. According to R. Ellis (1995), it might be difficult to exactly determine what forms learners are ready to learn. For example, many learners know how the simple present tense is constructed but may not know its different functions. They may know that it can be used to express habitual actions, but may not know that it can also be used to express general truth (e.g., "If ice melts, it becomes water."). Nassaji (1999) suggested that attention to the linguistic, functional or psychological complexity of the target form may also be helpful to determine what form should be selected, or at what stage of instruction it should be introduced in the classroom. This is not an easy decision because some forms that are linguistically easy, such as the third person singular -s, might not necessarily be easy to learn.

Learner Output during Structured Grammar-Focused Tasks

It has been suggested that if learners can discuss the language they are producing during task performance, such task talk will not only increase their consciousness of the relationship of form to meaning, thereby improving accuracy (Robinson, 2007), but it will also enable them to gain control over their learning (Swain, 2005) (see Chapter 7). Task talk produced during performance of the two types of structured grammar-focused tasks previously described allows learners to enhance their understanding of the target structures and, through negotiated interaction, to develop increased awareness of the target grammar feature (R. Ellis, Tanaka, & Yamazaki, 1994; Nobuyoshi & Ellis, 1993; Yuan & Ellis, 2003). Such a process-oriented approach explains the positive findings reported (R. Ellis, 2003; Fotos, 1993, 1994; Samuda & Bygate, 2008) on learner noticing and proficiency gains achieved solely through grammar-based task performance. It is also recommended, in the case of explicit task rule generation, that the results of the tasks performed by the groups are presented to the rest of the class and, if the teacher desires, the presentations can be followed by a formal discussion of the grammar point in the form of a mini-lesson.

Examples of Implicit and Explicit Structured Grammar-Focused Tasks

As mentioned, one type of structured grammar-focused task employs an implicit FonF during interactive task performance whereas another type has an explicit FonF (Fotos, 1993, 1994; Fotos & Ellis, 1991) since the target grammar structure itself comprises the task content. For example, pairs or groups of learners are asked to solve grammar problems such as adverb or indirect object placement on the basis of positive and negative information given on task cards. After listening to and writing down correct sentences, the learners then discuss the sentences and develop rules for the use of the target structure. Thus, even though the task contents are grammar problems, the learners must use the target language meaningfully to complete the activity. Again, the need to write English sentences and agree upon grammar rules promotes communicative use of the target language even though the learners speak the same L1 (Fortune, 2005). The following section presents sample classroom tasks of both types.

Activity 1. Prepositions of Location

The first task is an implicit structured grammar-focused task and consists of a picture of a living room. Working in groups of three or four, learners are given task cards with questions about the location of different items, such as a book, a table or a chair. The other learners answer the questions. The target structure is the use of prepositions of location, although this is not mentioned in the task, which appears to be purely communicative.

Activity 2. Different Forms of the Past Tense

A second implicit consciousness-raising task asks pairs or groups of learners to work together to reconstruct a past event that they have participated in, with the target structure being the past tense. They discuss and agree upon an event and create a story describing it, which they then present to the rest of the class. Again, although the target structure is L2 past tense usage, the task makes no mention of it. However, teachers may choose to follow task performance by pointing out L2 past tense uses and presenting a mini-lesson.

Activity 3. Discovering Rules About "If-conditional" Forms

This task can be either implicit or explicit. Working in groups of three or four, the learners read a dialogue in which if-conditionals have been put into italics (Fotos, 1995), and are then asked to make several questions each from the dialogue using *if*. The other group members answer the questions, as in the example below:

> Question: "What will happen if I don't study for the test?"
> Answer: "If you don't study for the test, you may not pass it."

The students then ask the other class members the questions they have made. If desired, the task can be followed by a mini-lesson on if-conditionals to promote increased noticing of the target structure.

Activity 4. Using an Information Gap Task to Generate Rules for Indirect Object Placement

In this explicit structured grammar-focused task, learners work in groups. Each student is given several sentences containing a target grammar structure, in this case, indirect object placement. They read their sentences to the members of their group and, after all sentences have been read and understood, the group attempts to generate rules for indirect object placement. Here is a sample task card (Fotos, Homan & Poel, 1994).

She asked her friend a question.
He offered snacks to the guests.
We bought many flowers at the store.
I cooked my family a wonderful meal.

The rules generated by the learners after all task cards have been read and discussed are that the indirect object may come before the direct object, but may also come after the direct object, or can occur in both positions with most short verbs. Learners may note that indirect objects usually occur as a prepositional phrase following the direct object in longer verbs. Each group then reports their rules to the rest of the class. Again, this may be followed by a mini-lesson expanding on the grammar rules presented.

Activity 5. Discovering Rules for Word Order in the Target Language

This explicit task compares word order in the learners' native language and the target language. Groups of three or four pupils are given two texts, one in the target language and one in the L1. The groups are then asked to mark the subjects and the verbs in the texts, comparing the position of the subjects and the verbs in the two languages. They then propose rules for the word order in the L1 and the target language to the rest of the class.

Activity 6. Discovering Rules for "For" and "Since"

The following task is adapted from R. Ellis (2002) and provides an example of an explicit structured grammar-focused task. Groups of learners are presented with sentences on task cards such as the ones below and are asked to determine when *for* is used and when *since* is used:

Ms. Smith has been working for her company for most of her life.
Mr. Jones has been working for his company since 1970.
Ms. Williams has been working for her company for 9 months.
Mr. Thomas has been working for his company since February.

The groups then develop rules to explain when *for* and *since* are used and present their rules to the rest of the class.

Alternatively, the learners can be presented with sentences that contain correct and incorrect instances of *since* and *for* such as the following.

I have read this chapter for five times.
I was at this school since 1998.
I have been in this room for 2 hours.
I haven't seen you for quite a long time.
I have been studying this lesson for two o'clock.

The learners can then be asked to determine which sentences are grammatically correct and which are grammatically incorrect. The learners then develop a grammar rule that explains the correct uses of *for* and *since*.

Activity 7. Noticing Adverb Placement (a Second Task for this Structure)

In this explicit task, the learners are told to work in groups and study the following sentences. They are given the following explanation of the sentences:

These sentences contain *adverbs,* words which describe the verb. Adverbs can occur in several places:

Yesterday he studied English.
We quickly ate lunch.
He studied for the test carefully.

But adverbs cannot occur in one location in the English sentence.

The groups must find the location in which adverbs cannot occur. To help them solve this problem, they ask and answer questions which contain sample adverbs.

Activity 8. A Relative Clause Task

Groups of learners are told that this explicit task is about making sentences with *who*, *whom*, *which* and *that*. They take turns reading task cards that give one rule and correct and incorrect sentences showing that rule. The student who reads the rule and sentences must then make his or her own sentence illustrating the rule. At the end, students write down the rules, and a sentence that illustrates each rule. They then present their work to the rest of the class.

The main goal of the above tasks is to develop the learners' explicit knowledge of the target structures. If so, the question becomes to what extent such tasks facilitate learners' communicative ability (R. Ellis, 2002). Ellis argued that such tasks do "not contribute directly to the acquisition of implicit knowledge, (they do) so indirectly" (p. 171). Ellis also noted that the development of implicit knowledge involves the following processes (p. 173):

1 *Noticing* (the learner becomes conscious of the presence of a linguistic feature in the input, whereas previously she had ignored it).
2 *Comparing* (the learner compares the linguistic feature noticed in the input with her own mental grammar, registering to what extent there is a "gap" between the input and her grammar).
3 *Integrating* (the learner integrates a representation of the new linguistic feature into her mental grammar).

According to Ellis, structured grammar-focused tasks contribute to the development of implicit knowledge by facilitating noticing and comparing. They may also assist integration, but do not result in it, as this process can only take place when learners are developmentally ready (see Pienemann, 1984).

However, if such tasks are followed by ample exposure to communicative activities containing the target structure, the learners will be more likely to integrate the target form into his or her implicit knowledge system. As research suggests (summarized in Samuda & Bygate, 2008), frequent exposure to the target structure in subsequent communicative activities not only increases awareness of the form but also assists processing and retention.

Skehan (1998b, p. 129) has proposed five principles for implementation of task-based instruction with a FonF which are particularly suitable for implementing structured grammar-focused tasks: (1) choose a range of problematic target structures; (2) choose tasks which meet the utility criterion, meaning that the structure is useful for competing that task; (3) select and sequence the tasks to achieve balanced goal development; (4) maximize the chances of focus on form through attentional manipulation; (5) use cycles of accountability to constantly evaluate learners' performance on how they do the task, achieved by having them present the tasks to the rest of the class.

Conclusion

The use of communicative tasks with target grammar structure as content presented implicitly or explicitly has been shown to successfully raise learner awareness of the target form. The studies of implicit and explicit structured grammar-focused task performance reviewed here (see Wong, 2005) have shown that the most task talk is produced if three features are built into the task. First, the tasks should be information gap tasks, where students have to exchange information. Second, the students should agree upon a task solution, and third, they should have a chance to think through what they are going to say, in order to plan their language. The goal of the structured grammar-focused tasks presented in this chapter is to draw learners' attention to form. They differ from unfocused communicative tasks, where the goals are only to promote negotiation of meaning and to facilitate comprehension or production of the message. Structured grammar-focused tasks also aim to promote negotiation about language forms by giving learners "grammar problems to solve interactively;" thus, the latter "has an L2 grammar problem as the task content" (Fotos, 1994, p. 325). As R. Ellis noted, consciousness-raising tasks should not be used as a replacement for communicative tasks in L2 classrooms but as a complement. The explicit form-focused component of consciousness-raising task makes them useful for communicative L2 classrooms with a heavy meaning-focused component and hence can be used to complement meaning-focused communicative tasks.

Questions for Reflection

1   What is the difference between implicit and explicit structured grammar-focused tasks? For what type of learners is each task type most useful? Why do you think so?
2   Design an implicit task for your classroom situation with a problematic grammar structure embedded. Decide how you would begin and end the class using this task. Would you teach the point in a mini-lesson? Why or why not?
3   Design a language task with a "real-life" component for learners in the EFL situation. Also incorporate a structure-focused component.
4   As teachers, how can we create tasks that work with different learner abilities? For example, both implicit and explicit focused tasks are useful learning tools given the right factors. Which task would be most useful for beginner students, intermediate students and more advanced students? Why?
5   Given classroom time constraints, is a task-based approach an effective choice for maximizing language learning? With regards to EFL contexts, how would you incorporate a task-based approach for students who are ultimately interested in passing a written exam?

Useful Resources

Cameron, B. (2007). *Opportunities in teaching English to speakers of other languages.* New York: McGraw-Hill.

This provides a useful introduction to teaching English in the EFL context for the beginning teacher, with definitions, acronyms, and advice on teacher training. The sections on creating curriculum, lesson plans and activities suitable for various cultures are especially useful.

Ellis, R. (2003). *Task-based language learning and teaching.* Oxford: Oxford University Press.

This book is a classic resource covering all types of language learning tasks and designs. Research, examples and task creation tips are included. Various task types are explained and examples are provided for different instructional contexts. The book presents numerous perspectives in order to give a balanced idea of what task-based learning does, and the areas in which this type of learning can excel and where it can fail. This text is not a guide for applying task-based learning in the classroom, but a book examining this type of learning, giving a clear insight into what task-based learning is all about.

Hewings, A., & Hewings, M. (2005). *Grammar and context: An advanced resource book.* London: Routledge.

This textbook was created in order to explore grammar and grammatical choices, and to examine how each of them functions within communication and context. The book contains a number of useful tasks as a way to facilitate the reader's learning. This text can be explored by section or as a whole, and is designed to engage the reader with understanding grammar, and how it is involved within a range of mediums and contexts.

Nunan, D. (2004). *Task based language teaching.* Cambridge: Cambridge University Press.

This is another classic resource on language tasks dealing with meaning-focused, real-life tasks, their development, use and outcomes. Nunan explains various task types, gives examples, and offers constructive hints for different functional contexts. The text is meant to equip teachers with both the theory behind task-based language teaching and a practical introduction to accompany it, including a task-based framework, an explanation of what makes up a "task," an account of the progression of research involved in this field, and the issues surrounding the integration of focus on form techniques in the classroom.

Samuda, V., & Bygate, M. (2008). *Tasks in second language learning.* New York: Palgrave-Macmillan.

This comprehensive book treats such topics as task development, research, and the interactions between research and practice and task development.

It is an excellent resource book since various task types are considered, designs are presented, and learner results after performance are discussed. Recent research is also presented to support task design.

Willis, J., & Willis, D. (2007). *Doing task-based teaching.* Oxford: Oxford University Press.

This compilation looks at what is possible in terms of innovation within L2 task-based instruction for both teaching and teacher training. The book examines the beliefs underlying the PPP (Presentation–Practice–Production) model of instruction in English language pedagogy and its perceived shortcomings. It then offers useful ideas about planning and implementing task-based instruction in L2 classrooms.

Chapter 7

Focus on Grammar through Collaborative Output Tasks

Introduction

In this chapter, we will consider collaborative output tasks, which refer to activities that are designed to push learners to produce output accurately and also consciously reflect on, negotiate, and discuss the grammatical accuracy of their language use. This method rests on the assumption that, during collaborative output activities, learners get collective help and guided support as a result of interacting with each other in order to solve linguistic problems and produce output accurately. We will first discuss the theoretical rationale for collaborative output. Then we will discuss collaborative output tasks and how they can be designed. We will also briefly review the empirical research that has examined their effectiveness. Finally, we will provide examples of these tasks that can be used in L2 classrooms.

Theoretical Rationale

Collaborative output refers to instructional options that push learners to produce output by performing tasks that require them to pay attention to both meaning and grammatical forms. The use of such tasks is motivated by a desire to integrate task-based student collaboration and output-based interaction in L2 classrooms. In this section, we will discuss two theoretical perspectives that bear directly on collaborative output: Swain's (1985, 1995) output hypothesis, which claims that learners need to engage in language production in order to increase their L2 proficiency, and the sociocultural theory of mind, which argues that learning is essentially social and that collaborative interaction is an important component of successful language learning.

Output Hypothesis

Input and output are both essential for L2 acquisition; however, the exact role of these processes has been disputed among SLA researchers. Krashen (1981, 1985), for example, has argued that language acquisition is mainly driven by comprehensible input, that is, target language that is understood by the learner. Krashen has contended that speaking and writing are just signs of learning and not the cause of learning. According to Krashen, one can basically acquire an L2 "without ever producing it" (Krashen, 1981, p. 107). Swain (1985, 1995) has argued that there are important roles for output in L2 acquisition and that although comprehensible input is essential, it is not sufficient for successful L2 acquisition. Thus, learners need to be provided with opportunities for output in both written and oral communication. According to Swain, output forces learners to move from semantic processing involved in comprehension to syntactic processing needed for production.

The argument for the role of output grew out of studies of content-based and language immersion programs in Canada. Findings demonstrated that mere exposure to meaningful content was inadequate for the acquisition of grammatical accuracy (e.g., Harley & Swain, 1984; Lapkin, Hart, & Swain, 1991; Swain, 1985, 1993). These studies have found that although immersion students are exposed to many hours of comprehensible input, their language performance is still inaccurate with respect to certain aspects of the L2. One reason for this, Swain has argued, is that learners in these programs do not have enough opportunities for L2 production, particularly production that pushes learners beyond their current level of interlanguage, what Swain called *pushed output.*

Swain (1993) distinguished three functions of output in L2 acquisition: (1) a noticing (or triggering) function; (2) a hypothesis testing function; and (3) a metalinguistic function. The noticing function proposes that when L2 learners are engaged in producing output, such as speaking and writing, they will become aware that they cannot say what they want to say. In other words, they will notice a hole or a gap in their linguistic ability (Doughty, 2001). When learners notice a hole in their linguistic ability, they become more conscious of the information provided in subsequent input; hence, they may benefit from it more effectively. It has also been suggested that such noticing is crucial for L2 acquisition because it triggers certain cognitive processes implicated in L2 learning, such as searching for new information or consolidating already existing knowledge (Swain, 1995). A number of studies have examined the noticing function of output and have provided empirical evidence for its existence and its relationship with L2 learning (e.g., Izumi, 2002; Izumi & Bigelow, 2000; Izumi, Bigelow, Fujiwara, & Fearnow, 1999; Swain & Lapkin, 1995).

The second function of output, according to Swain, is the hypothesis testing function. This function posits that output provides learners with opportunities for trying and testing out their hypothesis about how to express their meaning in an L2. When learners attempt to convey their message, they may try out different ways of saying the same thing or may come to recognize if their utterances are comprehensible or well-formed. If they cannot express their intended meaning, they may search their existing linguistic resources to find solutions, consequently modifying their original output. There is ample evidence from L2 interaction research that suggests learners are indeed able to modify their erroneous output in response to clarification signals in the course of interaction. In turn, this suggests that learners have been actively involved in hypothesis testing by trying out new modified linguistic utterances as a result of producing output and receiving feedback (Doughty & Pica, 1986; Gass & Varonis, 1994; Long, 1985; Pica, 1987, 1988). Swain (1995, p. 126) stated that "erroneous output can often be an indication that a learner has formulated a hypothesis about how the language works, and is testing it out."

The third function of output is its metalinguistic function. This claims that opportunities for output encourage learners to consciously reflect upon language, thinking about what to say and how to say it. Swain and Lapkin (1995) pointed out that output not only prompts learners to become conscious of their linguistics problems, it also raises their awareness of what they need to learn about their L2. In other words, "learners' own language indicates an awareness of something about their own, or their interlocutor's use of language" (Swain 1998, p. 68). Such reflective uses of language mediate L2 development by helping learners gain control over language use and also internalize their linguistic knowledge (Swain, 1997).

Output plays a number of other roles in language acquisition in addition to what is mentioned above. This includes enhancing fluency, providing opportunities for feedback, and also cultivating learners' communication strategies as a result of participating in conversational discourse. Output also assists acquisition by turning declarative knowledge (i.e., knowledge about language) into procedural knowledge (knowledge about how to use language) (de Bot, 1996). In addition, it provides learners with auto input (that is, output that feeds back into learners' linguistic system as input and become the source of new knowledge) (R. Ellis, 2003). Skehan (1998a, pp. 16–22) has summarized the contributions of output as follows:

1 *Output generates better input*: when learners speak and interact with an interlocutor, they have opportunities for meaning negotiation, which then leads to input which is more fine-tuned to the learners' level of competence.

2 *Output promotes syntactic processing*: when learners listen, they simply need to extract meaning from input, but when they speak, they also need to pay attention to the means by which meaning is expressed.

3 *Output helps learners test their hypotheses about grammar*: when learners produce output, they are in charge of making meaning. Therefore, they have to take risks, try out hypotheses, and look for the interlocutor's reaction or feedback.

4 *Output facilitates automatization of existing knowledge*: the development of automaticity requires ample opportunity for practicing the target linguistic form. Output provides learners with such form-focused practice.

5 *Output helps the development of discourse skills*: learning a language involves not only the development of an ability to produce sentence-level structures but also the development of skills to produce extended

discourse. This will not be developed unless learners participate in activities that require extensive production of discourse-based output.

6   Output helps learners "develop their personal voice" by focusing on topics that they are interested in.

Sociocultural Perspective

An important component of collaborative output is pair work. Theoretically, the use of collaborative activities in L2 classrooms is supported by a social constructivist perspective of L2 learning. According to this view, higher-order mental activities are all socially mediated operations. This mediation takes place through the use of various forms of physical and symbolic tools and artifacts, which allow us to establish a connection between ourselves and the world around us. In this view, an important tool of mediation is social interaction.

Current conceptualizations of a sociocultural view draw heavily on the work of Vygotsky (1978, 1986) and his ideas about how learning takes place in the mind. A number of concepts are central to the Vygotskian sociocultural theory. One is the notion of the Zone of Proximal Development (ZPD). The ZPD refers to "the distance between the actual developmental level as determined by independent problem solving and the level of potential development as determined through problem solving under adult guidance or in collaboration with more capable peers" (Vygotsky, 1978, p. 86). The notion of ZPD highlights the central role of collaboration in mediating learning and cognitive development. When learners collaborate within the ZPD, the act of collaboration pushes them towards higher levels of development, enabling them to learn what they are capable of learning (Nassaji & Swain, 2000). At every stage of the learning process, peers who negotiate within their ZPD are likely to reach a more sophisticated developmental level within their potential ability (Nassaji & Cumming, 2000).

Another key concept is the notion of scaffolding. Scaffolding refers to the supportive environment created through the guidance and feedback learners receive during collaboration (Donato, 1994). When learners collaborate with others, they master what they have not been able to master independently. This happens particularly when learners interact with a more capable person. In such cases, the less capable participant's language skills can be expanded and elevated to a higher level of competence. A point to note is that scaffolding is support that is not random, but rather is negotiated within the learner's ZPD. It is a guided support jointly "constructed on the basis of the learner's need" (Nassaji & Swain, 2000, p. 36). The importance of negotiated help over random help within the ZPD was explored by Nassaji and Swain (2000) in an experimental study in which ESL students were provided with different kinds of help from a tutor when learning English articles. The results revealed that scaffolding within the learner's ZPD in a collaborative fashion helped the learner to acquire the target language forms more effectively than help that was provided randomly and provided in a non-collaborative fashion. There are a number of other studies in the field of L2 acquisition that have examined the role of interaction in promoting scaffolding and have found evidence that scaffolding occurs in student–teacher interaction when the teacher adjusts feedback to suit learners' language level (e.g., Aljaafreh & Lantolf, 1994; Ohta, 2001) or when learners interact to solve linguistic problems during collaborative pair work (e.g., Lapkin, Swain, & Smith, 2002; Storch, 1998, 2001).

The third concept developed from a Vygotskian framework is the notion of regulation. According to Vygotsky, learning is both a social process and a process of moving from object-regulation to other-regulation to self-regulation. Object-regulation is a stage where the learner's behavior is controlled by objects in their environment. For example, at early stages of learning an L2, learners may be able to respond to only the stimuli that are available in here-and-now contexts. As they progress, they can respond to more abstract entities. Other-regulation refers to situations when the learner has gained some control over the object, but still needs the help or guidance of others. Self-regulation occurs when the learner becomes skilled and able to act autonomously.

The notion of regulation highlights two important ideas in sociocultural theory. First, it explains that new knowledge begins in interaction and becomes internalized and consolidated through interaction and collaboration. Second, it reveals the inherent connection between inter-psychological and intra-psychological (in thinking) functioning (Wertsch, 1985). In other words, it explains the transition from the inter-mental ability that is initially used in interaction to intra-mental ability (such as intentional thinking) that takes place inside the learner. This transition is evident when someone begins to act independently, showing control over his or her own behavior (Appel & Lantolf, 1994; Donato, 1994). A number of researchers have explored these mechanisms and have found evidence that collaborative interaction helps learners progress from lower to higher order mental functions (see Lantolf, 2000, for a review of these studies).

In short, sociocultural theory highlights the importance of interaction and collaborative work in the process of language learning. In this view, collaborative interaction mediates language learning. When learners collaborate with others, they can develop what they have not yet mastered independently and can also use and consolidate their existing linguistic knowledge. In particular, when interacting with more capable people or co-operating with their peers, a supportive context is created that helps the learner reach a higher cognitive level than what they are able to achieve when they work alone. In other words, new knowledge begins in interaction and also becomes internalized and consolidated through collaboration with others.

Collaborative Output Tasks

The importance of the role of output in L2 learning, as well as opportunities for collaborative negotiation, provides important arguments for incorporating tasks into language classrooms that meet these requirements. This can be achieved through collaborative output tasks, that is, activities that are designed to push learners to produce output collaboratively and also reflect on and negotiate the accuracy of their language production. Such activities are beneficial to L2 learners because when output is produced collaboratively, learners are not only pushed to use the target structure, but they will also get help from their peers when trying to make their meaning precise (Kowal & Swain, 1994; Swain & Lapkin, 2001; Swain, 2005). Collaborative output will also provide learners with opportunities to reflect on language consciously and to talk about and debate language forms, which raises their awareness of problematic forms. Swain and Lapkin (2001) noted that, through collaborative output, not only is meaning co-constructed but the language itself is developed as well. Swain further argued that such co-construction of language "allows performance to outstrip competence; it's where language use and language learning can co-occur" (1997, p. 115). In the following section we will describe several collaborative output tasks, including dictogloss, collaborative jigsaw, and text reconstruction tasks. We will then briefly review research that has explored how such tasks bring about beneficial effects for language learning, followed by activity examples.

Dictogloss

There are a variety of collaborative output tasks for L2 classrooms that elicit output and also promote discussion about language forms. One such task that has received much attention in current research is the dictogloss (Wajnryb, 1990). Dictogloss is a kind of output task that encourages students to work together and produce language forms collaboratively by reconstructing a text presented to them orally. Wajnryb defines such tasks as follows:

> Dictogloss is a task-based procedure designed to help language-learning students towards a better understanding of how grammar works on a text basis. It is designed to expose where their language-learner shortcomings (and needs) are, so that teaching can be directed more precisely towards these areas.
>
> (p. 6)

In a dictogloss, the teacher reads a short text at a normal pace while students jot down any words or phrases related to the content as they listen. Students then work in small groups or pairs to reproduce the text as closely as possible to the original text in terms of grammatical accuracy and cohesion. According to Wajnryb (1990), a dictogloss activity involves four stages:

1 *The preparatory stage*: this includes informing students of the aim of the task and what they are expected to do. It also involves a warm-up discussion of the topic and presentation and explanation of unknown vocabulary

in the text. At this stage, students are also organized into groups before they begin the task.

2 *The dictation stage*: the teacher reads the text twice at a natural speed. The first time, students listen to the text very carefully. The second time, they listen and take notes of important words or ideas related to the content.

3 *The reconstruction stage*: students work together in small groups and use their notes to reconstruct the text as accurately as possible. Students use the target language to discuss the accuracy of their language use. During this stage, the teacher's role is to monitor students' activities and provide feedback or language input.

4 *The analysis and correction stage*: the reconstructed text is analyzed, compared with the original, and corrected by students and the teacher together. At this stage, students discuss the choices they have made to become aware of their different hypotheses and solutions. The teacher will help students understand their linguistic problems and how to fix them.

The aim of a dictogloss task is not only to push learners to produce output collaboratively, but also to promote negotiation of form and meaning. There are a number of advantages of the dictogloss. First, it promotes verbal interaction in a realistic communicative context. To complete the dictogloss, learners need to communicate and help each other to reconstruct the passage. Participants should reconstruct the text as accurately as possible. This requires them to engage in extensive discussion about the appropriate lexical and grammatical forms. Thus, the task pushes learners to reflect on their own language output and get engaged in meta-talk, or talk about language. Since the task is collaborative, it encourages learners to pool their knowledge together and learn from each other. Because it is output-based, it enables them to find out what they know and what they do not know about the language. Thus, it raises learners' consciousness of specific aspects of language use.

The text used for a dictogloss can be an authentic text or a text that the teacher constructs or modifies. It would be helpful if the text contains several instances of a particular grammatical form, as this would facilitate learners' attention to form. A dictogloss task can be used with learners at all levels of language proficiency. Therefore, the complexity of the text varies depending on learners' linguistic level. For beginner level classes, for example, simpler and shorter texts can be used. For more advanced levels, longer and more linguistically sophisticated texts can be used. In all cases, the text should be carefully chosen in terms of the linguistic content and complexity. A text that is too difficult to understand may exert too much cognitive demand on learners, thus, negatively affecting their success in completing the task. A text that is too easy may not be able to push learners to produce output beyond their current level of linguistic ability. Thus, it may not be effective either. Furthermore, it is recommended that the text should be read twice to learners when using the dictogloss. However, the number of times a text is read can also be adjusted to suit learners' proficiency level. With lower-level learners, the teacher may read the text more than twice, and for more advanced learners, only once.

Reconstruction Cloze Tasks

Collaborative output tasks can also be designed in the form of reconstruction cloze tasks. A reconstruction cloze task is similar to a dictogloss in many respects. However, it differs from it in that during the reconstruction phase, learners receive a cloze version of the original text. In the cloze version, certain linguistic forms that are identified by the teacher as the focus of the task can be removed from the text. Thus, the task involves two versions of a text: an original version, which is read to students, and a cloze version. Students are then asked to reconstruct the text and also supply the missing items in the cloze version. The advantage of a cloze reconstruction task is that it requires students to reproduce specific target structures.

The procedure for completing the task is as follows:

1 The teacher reads the original version to students at a normal pace.
2 Students listen carefully for meaning and also jot down notes related to the content.
3 Students receive a copy of the cloze version of the text.
4 Students are asked to work in pairs to reconstruct the text and also to supply the missing words or phrases as correctly and as closely as possible to the original text.
5 Finally, students compare their reconstructed text with the original text and discuss the differences.

Text-editing Tasks

Another way of pushing learners to produce certain target items accurately is by using text-editing tasks. Text editing requires students to correct a text in order to improve its accuracy and expression of content. This task can be used either individually or collaboratively. However, when conducted collaboratively, the task has been shown to generate more attention to form and to promote the learning of targeted items more effectively (Nassaji & Tian, 2010; Storch, 2007). In this task, the teacher can read a text that contains instances of certain target forms and ask students to listen for comprehension (the reading comprehension component of the task is optional, but it is useful because it would ensure that the task has a meaning-focused dimension). Then the teacher gives learners a version of the task that contains errors. Learners are asked to edit the text collaboratively by making any changes they feel are needed in order to make the text as grammatically accurate as possible.

Collaborative Output Jigsaw Tasks

Collaborative output can also be designed in the form of jigsaw tasks. Jigsaw tasks are a kind of two-way information gap task in which students hold different portions of the information related to a task. Students should then share and exchange the different pieces of information to complete the task. According to Pica, Kanagy and Falodun (1993), for any jigsaw task to be effective, it should have the following characteristics: it should be goal oriented and it should generate negotiation of meaning. For a jigsaw task to be an effective output task, it should also be able to push learners to reproduce a particular linguistic target embedded in the tasks.

Collaborative jigsaw tasks are often designed in the form of segmented texts that students have to put together to create the original text. Pica, Kang, and Sauro (2006) described the steps in designing and implementing such tasks. A text that is authentic to students or related to the content of the course is selected. Then two versions of the text are prepared (e.g., versions A and B), with each version containing some sentences that are exactly the same as the sentences in the original passage. Other sentences are modified in that a target form in the original passage appears in a different form or order in the students' version. The task is then carried out as follows:

1 The teacher reads the original passage to students.
2 Pairs of students receive the modified versions of the passage, with one student receiving version A and the other version B.
3 Students attempt to choose the correct order of individual sentences as they appear in the original version.
4 Students attempt to choose between different sentences in versions A and B and find those that are the same in terms of grammatical accuracy as those in the original text. They also attempt to justify their choices.
5 Students compare their assembled passage with the original passage and identify any possible differences.

For a jigsaw task to become an output task, it could be designed to require learners to produce a certain linguistic form while completing the task. One way of doing so would be by adding a cloze component to the jigsaw task by removing some of the target forms in the students' version. Students would then attempt to complete the jigsaw by supplying the missing words. When completing the task, the students choose not only the correct order of the sentences but also attempt to choose the sentences that are the same as the ones in the original passage. They have also to supply the missing items. In all these steps, learners' attention can be drawn to the target forms. When learners attempt to order the sentences or to find the same sentence as in the original, their attention is drawn to form incidentally as a result of doing other activities. When they attempt to fill in the missing parts, their attention is drawn to forms more directly. In the last step, their attention is also drawn to form by comparing their text with the original and noticing the possible difference and gaps.

Effectiveness of Collaborative Output Tasks

A number of studies have investigated the use and effectiveness of different types of collaborative output tasks, including dictogloss, jigsaw, and other text-reconstruction tasks. In general, these studies have shown positive effects for promoting attention to form and L2 development. Kowal and Swain (1994), for example, examined whether collaborative output tasks such as dictogloss can promote learners' language awareness. They collected data from intermediate and advanced learners of French who worked collaboratively to reconstruct a reading text. Their results showed that when students worked together to reconstruct the text, they noticed gaps in their language knowledge, their attention was drawn to the link between form and meaning, and they obtained feedback from their peers. LaPierre (1994) studied the use of the dictogloss in Grade 8 French immersion classrooms. She also found a positive relationship between the linguistic forms that were correctly supplied during dictogloss interaction and learners' subsequent production of those forms. Nabei (1996) conducted a similar study with four adult ESL learners and found similar results. She found many instances where the activity promoted opportunities for attention to form, scaffolding, and corrective feedback. Swain and Lapkin (2001) compared the effects of dictogloss with jigsaw tasks with two groups of French immersion students. The focus was on how co-construction of meaning while doing the tasks promoted noticing aspects of the target language grammar. The researchers did not find any significant differences between the two types of tasks in terms of the overall degree of attention to form they generated, but they did find that the dictogloss led to more accurate reproduction of target forms than the jigsaw task. Pica et al. (2006) investigated the effectiveness of jigsaw tasks with six pairs of intermediate-level English L2 learners. Their results showed evidence for the effectiveness of such tasks for drawing learners' attention to form and also for helping learners to recall the form and functions of target items. In a recent classroom-based study, Nassaji and Tian (2010) examined the effectiveness of a reconstruction cloze task and reconstruction editing task for learning English phrasal verbs. Their results showed that completing the tasks collaboratively led to greater accuracy than completing them individually. However, collaborative tasks did not lead to significantly greater gains of vocabulary knowledge. There are also other studies that have examined and provided evidence for the role of collaborative output in L2 learning (e.g., García Mayo, 2002; Leeser, 2004; Storch, 1997, 2007). These studies have also shown beneficial effects for output tasks in terms of opportunities for a focus on grammar as well as social interaction.

Overall, the results of studies on collaborative output tasks have shown positive effects for task performance on learner grammatical accuracy. They have shown that through collaborative output, learners have opportunities not only to co-construct their meaning, but also to develop their linguistic and problem-solving skills.

Classroom Activities

Activity 1. Dictogloss

You, as the teacher, intend to teach or practice the use of relative clauses. You may choose a text such as the following, in which several instances of this structure occur.

Friendship

> We are always looking for good friends. These days it is hard to find true friends whom we can trust. Certainly, it is important to be considerate of those who care for us. However, a true friend is someone who is sincere and loyal, and is with us through tough times. We don't have to wonder if a friend, who is busy with a new partner and three kids, will have time to comfort us after a bad day. However, a true friendship is like a bridge that is built with planks of loyalty and fastened with nails of sincerity. It is that kind of connection that binds us together.

Procedures for completing the task:

1 *Preparation and warm-up*: discuss the importance of friendship and the different ways in which someone can be a friend. Examine the different characteristics of a good friend. Also, tell the class that they are going to hear a text on friendship. Ask them what they guess the text would include. Explain difficult vocabulary such as *trust, loyalty, sincerity,* and *considerate.*
2 *Dictation*: read the text at a normal pace. Ask learners to jot down the words related to the content as you read.
3 *Reconstruction*: ask learners to form groups of two or three and pool their resources to reconstruct the text as closely as possible to the original.
4 *Analysis and correction*: when they finish, ask learners to analyze and compare their versions. Go around the class and help learners to correct their errors. Do not show learners the original text until after the text has been compared and analyzed.

Activity 2. Reconstruction Cloze Tasks

The following task, adapted from Nassaji and Tian (2010), shows an example of a reconstruction cloze task. The task includes two versions of a text: an original version and a cloze version. The original text is in the form of a dialogue seeded with instances of a target structure (i.e., English phrasal verbs). The cloze version includes ten missing sections, four of which are related to target phrasal verbs. The other six relate to the other information needed to understand the text.

Original text

DAUGHTER: Hi, Mom. How are you?

MOM: Great. Guess what? I went to the mall yesterday and I met an old school friend. I haven't seen her since high school.

DAUGHTER: What does she do?

MOM: She's a lawyer and she's single. She got divorced years ago. Last year she met a nice man, but unfortunately they broke up.

DAUGHTER: Oh, that's too bad it didn't work out.

MOM: Yeah. She said he never wanted to do anything. He just liked to hang out with his friends.

DAUGHTER: He sounds immature.

MOM: I agree. It sounds like he needs to grow up.

Instruction: Please work in pairs and reconstruct the dialogue based on the one you just heard. Insert all the missing words and phrases needed.

DAUGHTER: Hi, Mom. How are you?

MOM: Great. – ? I went to the mall yesterday and I met –. I haven't seen her since high school.

DAUGHTER: What does she do?

MOM: She's a lawyer and she's –. She got divorced years ago. Last year she met a nice man, but unfortunately they –.

DAUGHTER: Oh, that's too bad it didn't –.

MOM: Yeah. She said he never wanted to do anything. He just liked to – with his friends.

DAUGHTER: He sounds immature.

MOM: I agree. It sounds like he needs to –.

Activity 3. Editing Task

The following provides an example of a text-editing task. The task includes two versions of a text: a correct version (version A) and a version with errors (version B).

1   The teacher reads the original text (version A) at a normal pace while students listen for meaning.
2   Students receive version B, and try to make any changes needed to the text based on what they just heard. (They try to make version B as grammatically accurate as possible.)

3 Students forms groups of two and then compare their responses and try to justify their choices.
4 Students compare their edited versions with the original version. The teacher provides feedback or explanations as needed.

Original text (version A)

There was a little girl who used to go camping with her parents every summer. They would travel by car for hours and reach a cabin just as the sun was going down. Before they even unpacked their belongings, her parents started a fire and roasted hot dogs and marshmallows. The girl used to go swimming with her mom every morning, and her dad would play with her until it was dark outside. When she wasn't playing she was chasing her pet dog around the cabin for hours. She never wanted to go away when camping was over, but always remembered that they would come back the next summer, and this made her very happy.

Text with errors (version B)

There was a little girl who use to go camping with her parents every summer. They would travel with car for hours and reach a cabin just as the sun was going down. Before they even unpack their belongings, her parents started fire and roast hot dogs and marshmallows. The girl used to go swimming with her mom every morning, and her dad will play with her until it was dark outside. When she wasn't playing she was chasing his pet dog around the cabin for hours. She never wanted to go away when camping was over, but always remembered that they would come back next summer, and this made her very happy.

Activity 4. Collaborative Output Jigsaw Task

The following provides an example of a collaborative output jigsaw task (modeled after Pica et al. (2006)) with a cloze component. The task includes two versions or an original text (e.g., versions A and B), with sentences that are the same as the sentences in the original passage and sentences which are modified. The target structure is the English simple past tense.

1 The teacher reads the original text.
2 One student receives version A and another version B.
3 Students try to choose the correct order of individual sentences as they appeared in the original version. They also compare different sentences in versions A and B to find which ones are the same and which ones are different in terms of grammatical accuracy from the original text. They also justify their choices.

4   Students try to supply any missing words and justify their choices.
5   Finally, students compare their constructed passage with the original passage.

Original text (version A)

There was a concert one night, and Bob wanted to go. He found tickets online and purchased them. However, he could not find anyone who wanted to attend the show with him. Bob asked people in his class, but they did not think they had enough money for accommodation. He asked people he worked with, but they were not able to get days off. When he was about to give up and sell his tickets to someone else, Bob received a phone call from his best friend, who told him that she was able to go with him.

Version given to student A

Sentence –
There was a concert one night, and Bob wanted to go.
   Sentence –
He found ticket online and purchased them.
   Sentence –
He asked people he work with, but they were not able to get days –.
   Sentence –
Bob asked people in his class, but they did not think they had enough money – accommodation.
   Sentence –
When he was about to give up and sell his tickets to someone else, Bob received a phone call from – best friend, who told him that she was able to go with him.

Version given to student B

Sentence –
There was a concert one night, and Bob wanted to go.
   Sentence –
He found tickets online and purchase them.
   Sentence –
He asked people he worked – but they were not able to get days off.
   Sentence –
When he was about to give up and sold his tickets to someone else, Bob received – phone call from his best friend, who told him that she was able to go with him.
   Sentence –
Bob asked people in his class, but they did not think they had enough money – accommodation.

Conclusion

In this chapter, we have discussed the use of collaborative output tasks. We discussed their theoretical underpinnings, studies that have investigated their effectiveness, and examples of such tasks. It can be concluded that collaborative output tasks such as dictogloss or output jigsaw tasks enable learners to produce output and also provide opportunities for scaffolding and feedback. They are also able to promote negotiation of form and enhance students' grammar skills. Thus, they can be considered as useful pedagogical tasks to be used in L2 classrooms. In addition to the output tasks we presented in this chapter, there are other types of tasks that teachers can use to integrate a focus on form with a focus on meaning in L2 classrooms. Another such task type is the grammar consciousness-raising task that will be discussed in the next chapter.

Questions for Reflection

1   According to sociocultural theory, collaborative activities provide learners with more learning opportunities than individual activities. Do you think this is always true? What are the different factors that may negatively or positively affect the effectiveness of collaborative group work?
2   This chapter discussed four kinds of collaborative output tasks: dictogloss, collaborative jigsaw tasks, cloze reconstruction tasks, and text editing tasks. Can you think of any other types of tasks that can be used as collaborative output tasks?
3   Design a collaborative output task for a specific group of students that you teach. What kind of text would you choose? What are your reasons for choosing that text? Which grammatical forms would you select to focus on in the task? Which criteria would you use in choosing the forms?
4   What are the differences between a dictogloss and a collaborative output jigsaw task? What are the advantages and disadvantages of each task?
5   What is your opinion on the use of a text-editing task as a collaborative activity? Such tasks involve designing texts with incorrect forms that students have to identify and correct. However, some people may argue that students should never see errors because if they see them, they learn the errors. What do you think?

Useful Resources

Lantolf, J. (2000). *Sociocultural theory and second language learning.* Oxford: Oxford University Press.
    This resource explores second language learning from a sociocultural perspective. It is aimed at expanding the ideas of sociocultural theory originally introduced by L. S. Vygotsky. The book explores the following concepts: mediated mind, genetic domains, unit of analysis, activity theory,

internalization and inner speech, and zone of proximal development. This is useful as a supplementary text for teachers to explore rationales behind different methods involving collaborative learning in second language classrooms.

Swain, M. (2005). "The output hypothesis: Theory and research." In E. Hinkel (Ed.), *Handbook on research in second language teaching and learning* (pp. 471–83). Mahwah, NJ: Lawrence Erlbaum Associates.
This chapter provides a detailed and up-to-date review of the various functions of output in second language learning. It begins with a discussion of the context in which the output hypothesis was introduced. It then presents each of the three functions of output: the noticing function, the hypothesis testing function, and the metalinguistic function. The chapter also reviews briefly the empirical studies that have examined the role of each of these functions in language learning.

Swain, M., & Lapkin, S. (2001). "Focus on form through collaborative dialogue: Exploring task effects." In M. Bygate, P. Skehan & M. Swain (Eds.), *Researching pedagogic tasks: Second language learning, teaching and assessment.* London: Pearson International.
This book chapter looks at communicative collaboration and its effect on task performance through a focus on form. This is useful for instructors by providing a perspective into collaborative discussion between learners, observing how communicative performance improves within a task-based framework through the discussion of ideas and the conscious attention paid to knowledge gaps, and the attempts to improve these gaps through multi-level background knowledge and the application of linguistic knowledge.

Wajnryb, R. (1990). *Grammar dictation.* Oxford: Oxford University Press.
This is a short handbook designed to introduce teachers to the dictogloss procedure, how to apply it, its aims, its stages, and its value in the learning environment. This book provides significant details related to the structure of this procedure, leaving the procedure open to variation and adjustment depending on both the needs of the students and the experience of the teacher. The book provides a wide variety of instructional activities suitable for teaching vocabulary and grammar.

Part III

Instructional Contexts and Focus on Grammar

Chapter 8

The Role of Context in Focus on Grammar

Introduction

In this chapter, we discuss the role of context in communicative focus on grammar. An important factor to consider in using FonF methods to teach grammar communicatively is the context of the instructional situation. For example, is it a second language or a foreign language context? In other words, is the target language a second language, spoken in the country where the learner resides, or is it a foreign language, studied in the learner's home country? There are a number of other contextual factors that have important implications for teaching grammar. Is the teacher a native speaker (NS) of the target language or a non-native speaker (NNS)? What about the age of the learner? Is the learner a child, able to learn language quickly and easily perhaps due to a language acquisition device (Chomsky, 1965), or is the learner post-puberty, or an adult, needing to learn through a more cognitive approach? How does the teaching of EFL fit in to the growing body of literature on World Englishes (Burns & Coffin, 2003; Jenkins, 2003)? Regarding the instructional situation, is the L2 learner studying in an immersion program with carefully selected content instruction in the L2 and considerable support for both L1 and L2 learning? Or is the learner mostly in the regular L2 program for NSs, with need for L2 instruction met through "pull-out" extra language classes? Or is the learner studying in a simplified content-based system taught in easy and simplified L2 with the goal of rapidly mainstreaming the learner into regular NS classes? Or is the L2 learner simply submerged in regular L2 classes with no L2 support at all?

The notion of context is multi-faceted, as it can be interpreted in many different ways. For example, context can also be considered to refer to the characteristics of the discourse events, the topic and the discourse type, as well as how the language learner is oriented to the target language and its teacher (Batstone, 2002). However, the variations of FonF according to the environmental contexts listed above have important consequences for teaching grammar. Therefore, they will be discussed in this chapter.

Second Versus Foreign Language Contexts

The Second Language Situation

Teaching a second language refers to second language instruction taking place in a country where the second language is spoken as the native language or L1. We will use English as a second language (ESL) as an example.

In the ESL context, as we have seen, English language learners have ample opportunities to encounter the L2 outside of the language classroom during their daily lives. Such encounters reinforce what has been learned in the classroom and make learners aware of the language functions required to live comfortably in the target culture. The classroom is only one of a variety of locations where the target language can be encountered. The current movement in English-speaking countries advocating the strong view of FonF, meaning to provide a purely implicit focus on grammar during communicative language teaching (Spada & Lightbown, 2008), followed by production opportunities and feedback on the correctness of the production, is now an important factor in ESL syllabus design since, as discussed throughout this book, the inability of communicative ESL teaching alone to promote high levels of accuracy in learners is now clear (Williams, 2005). However, teachers want to ensure that a return to grammar instruction is not the return of grammar-based syllabuses, drills, and other aspects of the grammar-translation approach (Nassaji & Fotos, 2004). As previous chapters show, there are a variety of implicit approaches to ensure that a focus on grammar can be performed in communicative contexts. This positive view of the role of implicit grammar instruction in the acquisition process is based on the assumption that ESL learners will encounter target grammatical forms that they have been made aware of both in their language classrooms and in their daily life. Such repeated encounters reinforce the FonF treatment by calling attention to the target structures, promoting awareness and processing.

ESL classroom activities may be task-based, with the target structures used frequently in the task, and a required component of the task solution (see Chapter 6), or be purely communicative materials with the target structure made conspicuous by bolding, underlining, stress in speaking, or by other means so that they are noticed during the activity, although not specifically addressed by the teacher. As mentioned, it has been shown (Nassaji & Fotos, 2004) that the effectiveness of such activities is greatly enhanced if learners are then required to undertake production tasks involving the target structures and have the opportunity to receive feedback on their correctness.

L2 learners may also engage in verbalization about language, what Swain has recently referred to as "languaging" (Swain, Lapkin, Knouzi, Suzuki, & Brooks, 2009), defined as discussions or self-reflection in the L1 about the L2, a process shown to lead to acquisition of target forms by promoting attention to them, thus enhancing processing. Languaging also consists of paraphrasing in the L1, inferencing, analyzing, self-assessment, and rereading (Swain et al.,

2009) and applies to both ESL and English as a foreign language (EFL) contexts as an important factor in developing the learner's concept of what is being learned (de la Campa & Nassaji, 2009). Form-focused instruction promotes languaging by making target forms more conspicuous to both ESL and EFL learners. As a result, their languaging often addresses the forms, particularly if done in group or pair work (see Li, 2001; Swain et al., 2009; Ueno, 2005).

The Foreign Language Situation

Whereas second language learners have abundant access to communicative target language use, this is not true for the foreign classroom, which, at best, serves only as a linguistic microclimate within the native culture (Rao, 2001). Foreign-language classroom contexts have been distinguished from second language classroom contexts in that native-like cultural and pragmatic competence is not a high priority in the former. To make it so would constitute a threat to the learners' own ethnic identities and also might not be favorably received by NS of that culture. Furthermore, some authors have commented (see Janicki, 1985) that NS teachers are likely to face social consequences when their linguistic and non-linguistic behavior does not comply with cultural sociolinguistic rules, for example, casualness in dress and manner in formal cultures, the use of obscenities, slang expressions, or very formal rather than standard language usage.

It has also been suggested that an appropriate model for L2 learners is that of a competent bilingual rather than a native-speaker model (Baker, 2006). This may well be the implicit model of many learners in foreign-language settings. The role relationships between teacher and student influence learning in a classroom. In the case of traditional approaches to language teaching, where the target language is perceived primarily as an object to be mastered by learning about its formal properties, the teacher typically acts as a "knower/informer" and the learner as an "information seeker" (Corder, 1977). In the case of innovative approaches (for example, communicative language teaching) where the emphasis is on the use of the target language in communicative situations, a number of different role relationships are possible, depending on whether the participants are doing role-play activities, or have a real-life purpose for communicating, as in information gap activities. The teacher can be a producer or a referee and the learner an actor or player. However, Corder noted that even "informal learning" inside the classroom may differ from that found in natural settings. As noted earlier, classroom learners often fail to develop much functional language ability, which may reflect the predominance of the knower/information seeker role set in classrooms.

Most English language instruction in the world occurs in the EFL situation, usually with teachers who are not NS of English. It is now recognized that English is the most widely taught, read and spoken language in the world

(Kachru & Nelson, 2006), and in many countries, grammar translation approaches continue to dominate. Consequently, NNS teachers suggest that the L2 learners' major problem is the lack of opportunities for communicative language use, not the lack of instruction on grammatical features (Braine, 2010).

Furthermore, in many countries the educational system has a central agency that organizes the curriculum, the content of courses, and even the textbooks to be used. Entrance to high schools and colleges is often based on comprehensive examinations with a strong English section. Thus, it is apparent why formalistic grammar instruction figures heavily in many EFL curriculums (Braine, 2010; Li, 2001). Unlike the ESL contexts, where learners have opportunities for exposure to meaningful language use in daily life, inside the EFL classroom, the teachers compensate by paying explicit attention to form. However, to enhance learning, they also need more communicative exposure, with implicit use of target forms.

Another complicating factor of communicative language usage in EFL is the large class size (Li, 2001; Sawar, 2001) and infrequent class meetings at many institutions (Fotos, 1998). As a result, the strong version of form-focused instruction, where learners are exposed to a target grammatical form only through communicative input, is usually not effective. As we have stressed, the implicit FonF approach depends on noticing the targeted form in communicative input, then having the opportunity to receive additional communicative input containing such forms, and being able to produce negotiated output containing the form. With large classes and few weekly meetings, such opportunities are often lacking in the EFL situation (Li, 2001; Rao, 2001). Therefore, more communicative input needs to be added to the already grammar-focused EFL classrooms. On the other hand, since learners in second language classrooms already have ample exposure to communicative input outside the classroom, the FonF methods in these contexts can be modified so that there is more form-focused instruction in conjunction with communicative instruction in the classroom. This, for example, can be achieved by adding formal mini-lessons before communicative activities to raise learners' awareness of the target form. Studies (summarized in Braine, 2010; R. Ellis, 2003; Nassaji & Fotos, 2004; Ueno, 2005; Williams, 2005) have found that L2 learners from communicative classes supplemented by teacher-fronted grammatical explanation, learner output opportunities, and subsequent correction of learner output errors, showed significantly greater accuracy in the instructed grammar forms than learners from classrooms with no instruction, feedback or output requirements. On the other hand, the integration of communicative input with form-focused strategies has led to better performance among foreign language learners. This has been found to be especially true when the teachers are NNS of English (Braine, 2010).

It has also been found that NNS teachers of English in EFL settings often use the L1 for formal instruction prior to engaging in L2 communicative activities (Li, 2001). Such uses of L2 can also be helpful, and as noted earlier, can be considered a form of languaging. A recent study (de la Campa & Nassaji, 2009) examined the amount, the purpose, and the reason for L1 use in foreign language classrooms, concluding that teachers tended to use their L1 most frequently for instructional purposes, including explaining difficult grammatical concepts, translating lexical meanings, and providing instructions for communicative tasks and activities. These findings suggest that the L1 is an important pedagogical and social tool in the foreign language context and can enhance target language learning (see also Colina & García Mayo, 2009). Although this is not a possibility where the teacher and learners do not share the same L1, in contexts where they do, such as in many foreign language classrooms, the L1 serves as an important aid for grammar teaching (Braine, 2010; Jenkins, 2003). As mentioned, mini-lessons on the target grammar structures delivered in the L1 prior to L2 activities, and summative L1 reviews of the problematic grammar structures enhance the learners' understanding of the target grammar forms, especially if the activity is then followed by output-based requirements and corrective feedback (Braine, 2010; Nassaji & Fotos, 2004).

In regard to these results, research on the use of advance organizers (Ausubel, Novak, & Hanesian, 1978) or meta-explanations of the material to be covered prior to the lesson suggests that formal preparation of learners before they are exposed to new L2 grammar forms enhances their acquisition of the forms (see reviews in Braine, 2010; R. Ellis, 2005; Nassaji & Fotos, 2004). Furthermore, in keeping with many EFL cultural traditions (Li, 2001; Rao, 2001), the use of summative activities—in this case, after communicative language studies containing the target structure—reviewing the different ways that the target form was used to create meaning (Fotos, 2005) also encourages learner awareness of the structure. In terms of explicit EFL form-focused grammar instruction, as noted, mini-lessons in either the L1 or the L2 (Mizumoto & Takeuchi, 2009; Spada & Lightbown, 2008) before performance of explicit task-based (Fotos, 2002) or explicit reading activities, followed by a wrap-up session again calling attention to the target structure as used in the activity, are suitable for many EFL contexts (Braine, 2010).

Implicit instruction in the EFL situation is similar to the ESL situation and consists of multiple exposures to the target form that has been made conspicuous so that it is noticed by the learner. This is followed by output exercises that require production of the form, followed by feedback on the output, so that the learners become aware of the target forms' use and correctness.

Form-focused reading and vocabulary activities are particularly suitable for many EFL situations because of the cultural emphasis on comprehension and translation skills (Braine, 2010; Fotos, 2005; Nassaji & Fotos, 2004). As noted in Chapter 3 on input enhancement, reading material can be highlighted so that the target structure is conspicuous while learners are reading for meaning. Listening activities can also contain multiple uses of the target structure. Prior to such activities, teachers employ the advance organizer (Ausubel et al., 1978) as an orientation to the coming activity, explaining its purpose and procedures and noting its target structures. This is often followed by special tasks or pair work (see Chapter 7) aimed at making target grammar forms salient to learners through communicative activities. The tasks are designed to increase learner awareness of how the embedded target structures are used in context, yet are communicative since learners are engaged in meaning-focused interaction (R. Ellis, 2005; Fotos, 1993, 1998; Nassaji & Fotos, 2004). Again, languaging in the L1 about L2 structures, particularly when done in group/ pair work, can enhance noticing of the target forms (Swain et al., 2009).

Non-Native Speakers Versus Native Speakers: World Englishes

Another factor that distinguishes many EFL contexts is the language background of the teacher. In this connection, the role of the NNS teachers versus NS teachers has received much attention. Because of the widespread teaching of English throughout the world and its use as an international language in multilingual contexts where speakers of various L1s meet and use English to communicate, the prevalence and importance of the NS teacher of English have declined (Jenkins, 2003). It has been suggested that "the future status of English will be determined less by the number and power of its native speakers than by the trends in the use of English as a second language" (Graddol, 1999, p. 62). A key concept in the decline in importance of the NS is the recognition that NSs do not have a more profound access to understanding the language and are not necessarily more reliable informants or teachers than NNSs (Li, 2001). Furthermore, they often lack knowledge of the local culture and select classroom materials and activities that are a poor match for learners' cultural norms and learning styles (Li, 2001; Rao, 2001; Holliday, 2001). One survey of learner attitudes towards NS and NNS teachers of English (Hertel & Sunderman, 2009) notes that, although the research is often anecdotal, the trend is for NNS teachers to be regarded as preferable for teaching courses such as reading or composition since they have the following distinct advantages over NSs: They serve as models of successful L2 learners, they teach strategies that they have used themselves, they have detailed linguistic knowledge that many NS teachers lack (Medgyes, 1992), and they can use the L1 to explain difficult points (de la Campa & Nassaji, 2009). It has also been emphasized (Holliday, 2001; Li, 2001) that although NSs have been believed to be superior to NNSs as teachers, they are, in reality, disadvantaged because they often lack explicit knowledge of English grammar and are unable to provide the necessary detailed explanations of grammar points, especially in the L1, and, as mentioned, often lack knowledge of the local culture and the expectations that learners have in the classroom (Holliday, 2001; Rao, 2001). While learners may want NS teachers because of their superior knowledge of pronunciation and the target language culture, they are not necessarily seen as superior in grammatical knowledge or in the ability to teach grammar (Braine, 2010; K. Brown, 2001).

This topic leads to a discussion of the concept of World Englishes, a term indicative of the changing role and function of English globally (K. Brown, 2001). World Englishes refers to a theoretical framework, often called the World English paradigm (Kachru, 1992), which holds that: (1) there is a repertoire of models for English, not only the English spoken in the UK, North America, Australia or New Zealand; (2) localized versions of English, such as the type of English used in India or Singapore, have valid pragmatic bases; and (3) English now belongs to the nations and peoples who use it as a second language or *lingua franca*, not exclusively to countries such as the UK, Australia, or North America where it is the native language (K. Brown, 2001; Jenkins, 2003). This concept has greatly supported recognition of the worth of NNS teachers (Braine, 2010). Thus, NNS teachers may well be more effective at form-focused instruction of grammar than NS teachers.

EFL Learner Proficiency Level

The level of the learner is another factor to consider in teaching grammar in different contexts, for example, with advanced learners who want more NS cultural information and collocation usage than beginning or intermediate learners. Again, although their fluency and cultural knowledge are appreciated by learners, NSs teachers have not been perceived as superior in grammatical knowledge (Jenkins, 2006). Thus, both NSs and NNSs are now seen to have strengths and weaknesses with regard to English teaching ability (Hertel and Sunderman, 2009).

Another consideration to make when evaluating learner proficiency in various contexts is evidence that learners tend to pass through fixed developmental sequences. Based on his studies of German learners of English, Pienemann (1989) developed a teachability hypothesis, suggesting that, while certain developmental sequences are fixed and cannot be altered by grammar teaching, other structures may respond to instruction. According to Pienemann, it is possible to influence development by form-focused instruction if grammar teaching coincides with the learner's readiness to move to the next developmental stage (Lightbown, 2000). Recent suggestions on the place of grammar in the L2 curriculum, particularly in classrooms with a communicative focus (e.g., R. Ellis, 2005), take these considerations into account. It has been noted that more proficient learners are more responsive to form-focused instruction because they notice the structures and are more able to be aware of feedback and make the necessary corrections in response (Baker, 2006). For example, in Chapter 3 we discussed an implicit form of focus on grammar called input flood. The effectiveness of this strategy seems to be highly dependent on learners' level of language competence. As Batstone and R. Ellis (2009, p. 187) pointed out, even if a feature is highly frequent in the input, learners may not notice it if "their current interlanguage does not contain a representation of this feature."

Studies have shown that there is a strong relationship between the effectiveness of FonF and language proficiency (Nassaji, 2010; Williams, 2001). It is also suggested that there is an interaction between language proficiency and types of FonF (see previous chapters for a discussion of the types). Nassaji (2010) found that although beginner and intermediate learners benefited more from preemptive FonF than reactive FonF, advanced level learners benefited equally from both types of FonF. Also, advanced level learners benefited significantly more from reactive FonF than less advanced learners. As Nassaji explained, if reactive FonF is more implicit than preemptive FonF, a positive response in advanced level learners suggests that language proficiency is affected more by implicit feedback more than explicit feedback. Perhaps explicit knowledge resulting from explicit feedback is not influenced to the same degree by learners' developmental constraints or readiness as implicit knowledge is (R. Ellis, 2005). As learners become more proficient, their automaticity in language use will also develop. Due to higher levels of automaticity, advanced level learners can devote more attentional resources to FonF. Thus, they may be better able to notice targeted form than less advanced learners (Nassaji, 2010). The results of other studies (e.g., Iwashita, 2001; Mackey & Philp, 1998; Williams, 2001) also support these conclusions. For example, Iwashita (2001) found that L2 learners' level of language proficiency impacted both the quality and quantity of their interactions, including the degree to which they were able to modify their output during interaction. Mackey and Philp (1998) also found that learners' linguistic ability was related to the degree to which they benefited from the provision of recasts in student–teacher interaction.

The Age of the Learner

Another context-related factor relevant to understanding form-focused instruction is the age of the learner. Traditionally L2 learning has been considered to be constrained by maturational factors, making it hard for older learners to reach a native-like mastery of the language (Baker, 2006). This view relates to what some people accept as Chomsky's theory of the language acquisition device (LAD) within the human brain (Chomsky, 1965). Conceiving of language as an innate capacity of the human mind and believing that mental structures exist which form the preconditions for language development, Chomsky held that there is a basic grammar system wired into the brain, the parameters of which are set according to what language the child is exposed to. This is a nativist theory of language acquisition and is not universally accepted, but is supported by the fact that children who learn the L2 in childhood often achieve a higher proficiency than those who learn it afterwards, especially in the area of pronunciation (Baker, 2006). Regarding L2 acquisition, it has also been proposed that, as in L1 acquisition, there may be a critical period for second language development. This L2 critical period hypothesis suggests that there is a time in childhood when the brain is especially capable of success in L2 learning. It has been suggested (Baker, 2006) that the critical period ends somewhere around puberty so that L2 learning which occurs after the critical period is not based on innate biological structures but more on cognitive learning abilities. This L2 critical period hypothesis has received support from several studies (see the review in Baker, 2006), and even though a number of researchers have suggested that high levels of L2 attainment may be possible for older learners (Mackey & Silver, 2005), it is generally thought that younger learners—those who have not reached puberty—are superior to older learners in their ultimate levels of L2 attainment.

Thus, there are two opposite views that have been proposed, both supported by research (see reviews in Baker, 2006; Lightbown & Spada, 1999). One view is that the younger the child is, the better he/she learns the target language. On the other hand, older children and young adults might learn a language more effectively and quickly than younger children because of their superior cognitive ability and their ability to process metalinguistic instruction (Nassaji & Fotos, 2004). For example, a 14-year-old has better processing skills than a 5-year-old, so less time may be required to learn the L2 (Baker, 2006; see also Altarriba & Heredia, 2008; Lightbown & Spada, 1999). Researchers investigating classroom interaction have also discussed the limited attention span of younger children as a barrier to L2 learning. Lyster's (2001) study of French immersion classroom learners aged 9 to 11 suggested that such young children were not able to recognize feedback as negative evidence correcting their errors. Proficiency levels in young students is also a factor. If learners are beginners, regardless of age, presenting and practicing form-meaning correspondence in context is an optimum strategy (Celce-Murcia, 1991). However, if learners are at the intermediate or advanced level, form-related feedback and correction should also be provided for them to progress.

The length of exposure is also a critical factor (Baker, 2006) to consider. Learners who start studying an L2 in elementary school and continue to study it through high school achieve higher proficiency than those who start their study later and end their study sooner. So time on task is important. For example, it has been widely observed that young children from immigrant families eventually learn to speak the language of their new community with near native-like fluency, but their parents rarely achieve high levels of mastery. Although some adult L2 learners can communicate successfully in the L2, for many, differences of accent, word choice, or grammatical features distinguish them from NSs and from L2 speakers who learned the language while they were very young (Lightbown & Spada, 1999). In majority language cultures, the pressure is to learn the L2 as soon as possible to live and work in the new culture. Again, because of the critical period hypothesis, it is suggested that children are more successful than adults and are thus often interpreters for their parents (Baker, 2000). Trilingualism may also be common. Here a child hears two languages at home and a third in school. Thus, bilingualism is thought to favor the acquisition of a third language (Baker, 2000, 2006).

In addition, younger learners in informal environments may have more time to devote to learning the L2. They often have more opportunities to hear and use it in situations where they do not experience strong pressure to speak fluently and accurately. Furthermore, their early imperfect efforts are often praised or, at least, accepted. On the other hand, older learners are often in academic situations that demand more complex L2 use and the expression of complicated ideas. Older learners may therefore be embarrassed by their lack of mastery of the L2 and may develop a sense of inadequacy after experiences of frustration in trying to say what they mean.

In educational research, it has been reported that learners who began studying the L2 at the primary school level did not do better over time than those who began in early adolescence (Baker, 2006). In addition, there are many anecdotes about older learners (adolescents and adults) who have reached high levels of proficiency in a second language (Baker, 2006). Thus, as mentioned, the optimum age of the learner remains inconclusive, with general evidence favoring the younger learner and an implicit FonF approach.

Regarding very young learner instruction, one author (Vaezi, 2006) described an ideal language learning environment where classroom rules are used, the learners are shown what to do by teacher modeling, the lessons are well-planned and consistent, and accuracy is a goal, but not at the expense of a relaxed and motivating classroom atmosphere, with implicit form-focused instruction. Story-telling, songs and games are strongly recommended, as well as pictures and videos. Thus, attractively designed, implicit, real-life, form-focused tasks which provide young ESL learners with the functional language forms needed for their new life are strongly recommended (Altarriba & Heredia, 2008). Again, such tasks should be followed by requirements for the learners to output the form and to receive feedback on the correctness of their output, although, as mentioned, younger children may not respond to corrective feedback by becoming aware of the correct form. Consequently, there is no conclusive evidence supporting the optimum age of L2 learners. Many factors intervene although the best time has been suggested to be between three and seven years old, before the onset of puberty (Baker, 2006).

After Puberty

Another aspect of the age of the learner relates to critical period concerns. As some suggest, after puberty the primary way for learners to master the L2, cognitive processes come into play. Cognitive processing models (Ausubel et al., 1978) were developed at the same time as Chomsky's nativistic theories and supported rather than disagreed with them. Whereas behaviorist psychology viewed language learning as a set of habits gained through conditioning, cognitive psychology considered language learning to be a creative activity, using mental processes in a conscious, analytical manner. Here, the system of a language is taught through formal grammatical explanations and analysis, and through cognitive exercises, including translation (Mizumoto & Takeuchi, 2009), that involve the understanding of meaning (DeKeyser & Juffs, 2005). As mentioned in previous sections, cognitive psychologist Ausubel (Ausubel et al., 1978) developed two concepts for education: (1) the advance organizer, presenting introductory material ahead of the learning task, explaining, integrating and interrelating the material in the learning task with previously learned material; and (2) subsumption, a review which connects previously learned material with the new material so that the new ideas are organized and more effectively stored within existing knowledge hierarchies.

In terms of explicit form-focused instruction, communicative exposure to target forms, preceded by an explanation of the forms and followed by a summary can be considered effective for L2 learners (Nassaji & Fotos, 2004). The features of the speech event, whether written or spoken, help learners map form and function, help develop pragmatic knowledge and make the new forms accessible (Batstone, 2002; DeKeyser & Juffs, 2005; Mizumoto & Takeuchi, 2009). Again, these activities can be followed by output-based activities requiring production of the forms, and teacher/peer feedback on the correctness of form use. Thus, form-focused language tasks for any age or level of learner can push the learners' output to new levels of accuracy in use of target grammar structures.

Classroom Learning Environments: Submersion, Immersion, Pull-out, and Sheltered English

A final contextual consideration is the mode of instruction of L2 learners. Will the learners study content material in an immersion environment entirely in the L2 through a carefully organized program strongly supporting both L1 and L2 development (Baker, 2006; Beardsmore, 1993)? Will L2 learners study mainly in the L2, with supplementary L2 classes delivered by pulling them out of regular classes to take ESL lessons? Will the ESL learner study content and L2 material in greatly simplified L2, often called a sheltered English program (Baker, 2000, 2006), with the goal of integrating them into regular classrooms within several years? Or will the L2 learner simply be plunged into regular L2 content classes with NS learners, without L2 instruction or assistance (a situation that has often been termed "sink or swim" by teachers)?

Regarding the latter, deemed the worst way to learn the L2 (Baker, 2006), a study of language minority learners who were placed in L2 classrooms with no L2 instruction or support (Vaipae, 2001) noted that nearly all of the older learners failed to learn the L2 and merely stayed in school until they were old enough to drop out. Very little target language learning took place in the submersion situation because of the lack of instruction in the target language. Other studies of submersion classrooms have reported similar findings (Baker, 2006; Harklau, 1994). Thus, submersion is considered to be the most ineffective context for target language acquisition (Baker 2000, 2006; Harklau, 1994) because the learner receives no instruction in the target language of any kind.

Immersion programs, thought to be the optimum situation for target language learning, have been extensively studied by researchers such as Swain and her colleagues (e.g., Lapkin & Swain, 2000, 2004; Lapkin, Swain, & Shapson, 1990). Although learner comprehension of the target language was excellent, because of the lack of output and feedback opportunities (Swain, 1993) promoting error correction, the learners continued to make a number of grammar errors, despite spending years in the immersion programs. As discussed in Chapter 7, this led to Swain's "pushed output" hypothesis (e.g., Swain, 1993, 1995). As we have seen, peer or teacher feedback on the accuracy of their output has also been shown (Batstone, 2002; Lyster, 2004; Nassaji & Swain, 2000) to increase learner awareness of the correct target forms (Swain, 1993, 2005; Swain & Lapkin, 2001; Lyster, 2004), and to assist their processing and acquisition. Many immersion programs also teach learners their L1 in regular language classes and use form-focused instruction to instruct them on both the grammar of the target language and their own L1 to promote high levels of accuracy (Lyster, 2007).

Thus, to summarize, effective implicit form-focused instruction in immersion contexts requires opportunities for noticing the target form, development of language awareness through making forms conspicuous, the provision of output opportunities to practice the form, and subsequent feedback on form correctness (Batstone, 2002; Nassaji & Swain, 2000; Lyster, 2004) followed by opportunities for correction of errors. Explicit instruction on target forms before and after communicative activities can enhance learner awareness as well.

The same considerations apply to "pull-out" situations, where L2 learners are removed from regular classrooms to study the target language. This situation has not received favorable reviews (Baker, 2006; Harklau, 1994). The limited and occasional instruction was not sufficient to allow L2 mastery, and support teaching in "Sheltered English," that is, teaching content courses in simplified target language with supporting classes of target language instruction as a supplement (e.g., Harklau, 1994; Vaipae, 2001), with the goal of mainstreaming the learners within a few years (Baker, 2006). This again was found to be an inadequate way of developing the necessary academic language proficiency in the L2 that would allow learners to succeed in classrooms with NSs because of the lack of sufficient instruction.

Conclusion

In reviewing the various contexts for target language instruction, it has been shown that both implicit and explicit form-focused instruction are recommended as effective pedagogy to promote L2 acquisition following the activities suggested in previous chapters. In the ESL situation, implicit form-focused instruction should be accompanied by opportunities for learner output and feedback on this output so that they can become aware of their limitations as to production goals, thus enhancing their awareness and need of the necessary correct forms. In both ESL and EFL situations, talk in the L1 has been validated as an important method to increase awareness of problematic forms. Explicit form-focused activities may be preceded and followed by formal explanations of target forms in the L1, as may implicit form-focused activities, with target forms made conspicuous through manipulation of the presentation material. Except for very young learners, the success of both implicit and explicit form-focused instruction is strongly dependent on the provision of output opportunities and subsequent feedback on the correctness of the output, often with requirements for output modification based on the results of the feedback, this pushing the learner further along the interlanguage continuum. Activities presented in previous chapters are recommended as a means to achieve this in different instructional contexts.

As we mentioned in Chapters 1 and 5, there are a number of other learner-related variables that affect the choice of teaching strategies, such as learners' motivation, attitudes, educational background and experience, and their learning styles and strategies. Thus, effective grammar teaching needs to take into account such individual learner differences.

Questions for Reflection

1   Discuss the major differences between second and foreign language learning. How is a communicative approach to teaching grammar useful in an EFL classroom where opportunities to use the language do not exist, or where the student's goals may have nothing to do with communicative competence?
2   Why is the NS teacher no longer viewed as essential for effective language teaching in the foreign language situation? What are the strengths and weaknesses of a NS teacher in various cultures? What can a NS teacher do to ensure classroom effectiveness?
3   Discuss the role of age in language learning. Who are better language learners, children under the age of seven or older? What is the role of puberty? How are languages learned after puberty?
4   Discuss the different types of classroom L2 learning environments. Which is seen as optimal and why? How can you justify the use of grammar-focused activities at beginner and intermediate levels?
5   In an EFL situation where high school students are planning on attending a foreign university in the US or Canada, what type of syllabus do you think would be most beneficial?

Useful Resources

Baker, C. (2000). *A parents' and teachers' guide to bilingualism*. Clevedon: Multilingual Matters.

This is an extremely practical, user-friendly guide to issues in bilingualism and how to promote it in the family, especially when family members speak an L1 and are living in an L2 culture. A number of approaches, techniques and activities are presented for families that are attempting to raise their children bilingually.

Baker, C. (2006). *Foundations of bilingual education and bilingualism* (4th edn.). Clevedon: Multilingual Matters.
In this classic book on bilingualism, Baker describes the cultural, social, psychological, educational and political concepts of bilingualism, offering suggestions for improvement in each area. He goes into depth on both theoretical concerns and practical issues, making this an indispensable handbook for teachers.

Burns, A., & Coffin, C. (Eds.). (2003). *Analysing English in a global context: A reader.* Macquarie: The Open University.
This edited resource book also provides various opinions on the teaching and learning of English worldwide, with a number of practical suggestions for curriculum design and activity implementation in various countries. Teachers will find the suggested activities useful in a variety of cultural settings.

Cameron, B. (2007). *Opportunities in teaching English to speakers of other languages.* New York: McGraw-Hill.
This provides a useful introduction to teaching English in the EFL context for the beginning teacher, with definitions, acronyms, and advice on teacher training. The sections on creating curriculum, lesson plans and activities suitable for various cultures are especially useful. The wide range of activities will appeal to teachers in a variety of settings, and the descriptions of how to use them are extremely useful.

Jenkins, J. (2006). *World Englishes: A resource book for students.* London: Routledge.
This book provides an introduction to the concept of World Englishes, the use of English as a world language, and provides a range of opinions on the subject, which can be used for discussion themes in advanced classes. A wide variety of situations are discussed in depth to inform teachers of the complex nature of World Englishes.

Chapter 9

Conclusion

Focus on Grammar in L2 Classrooms

The aim of this book has been to examine current developments in the teaching of grammar communicatively. As we have emphasized, the traditional grammar-based approaches that still often dominate foreign language situations have been challenged by the overwhelming demand for superior communicative ability in the target language. In the current global economy, communicative excellence in foreign languages is now regarded as essential for business, and learners are increasingly expecting to graduate from university with spoken and written fluency in the target language they have been studying. Compared to the purely communicative approaches of the past that did not address grammar in any way, L2 teachers, teacher educators, and researchers now recognize the importance of grammar instruction for accuracy in the target language and emphasize the need to incorporate form-focused instruction in communicative language teaching. The research findings summarized in the previous chapters have strongly supported this necessity.

A recurrent theme in this book is how current SLA theory and research can inform communicative grammar instruction. Our focus is largely on instructional options derived from that research. We began with an overview of the changes in grammar teaching over the years, and then examined a variety of approaches for classroom teaching in subsequent chapters. In particular, we have examined and illustrated the use of six theoretically and empirically motivated instructional options proposed to integrate grammar instruction and meaningful communication. The options included processing instruction, textual enhancement, discourse-based grammar teaching, interactional feedback, grammar-focused tasks, and collaborative output tasks. In each chapter we presented an option and its underlying theory and research. We also included examples of activities to illustrate how the option could be implemented in the classroom. However, in any discussion of grammar teaching, we must be careful not to over-simplify the issue, and note that there is no single answer as to how to treat grammar in L2 classrooms (Stern, 1992). Furthermore, we should keep in mind the complexity of the relationship between theory, research, and practice. Thus, in this section, we make a number of concluding remarks that are important to consider when dealing with teaching and learning grammar in L2 classrooms.

Point 1: Not all Grammar Forms and Structures Respond Equally to Instruction

As discussed throughout this book, there is now a general consensus that form-focused instruction facilitates the acquisition of L2 grammatical forms. However, this observation should not be taken to suggest that there is an inherent and directional relationship between language learning and language instruction. Language learning is a highly complex process, involving the interaction of a host of factors. Certainly, not all learners benefit equally from similar instructional strategies, nor do all features respond equally to instruction. As suggested by a number of SLA researchers (e.g., Doughty, 2003; R. Ellis, 2008; Lightbown, 2004; VanPatten, 2002a), while some language forms may be learned while learners' focus is primarily on the message, there are other forms that may need more focused instruction. For example, some grammatical forms that have low frequency or salience in the input, such as function words or certain morphological features, may be harder to notice in the input (see also Chapters 2 and 3). These features may need more focused instruction. There are also other factors that may influence the relationship between instruction and learning such as the complexity of the target form and the influence of the L1 (Spada & Lightbown, 2008). Again there is no straightforward relationship between linguistic complexity and learning. Some features may be linguistically easy, such as singular-s, but they are not easy to learn. Similarly, instruction is needed in cases where the difference between L1 and L2 provides students with non-target-like information about a particular structure in the L2. An example would be learning adverb placement in English by French native speakers. For example, an English learner of French may produce erroneous utterances such as "He is driving fast the car" based on L1 interference. In such cases, exposure to the target language input cannot help the learner to overcome the error because such utterances are ungrammatical in the target language. Thus, the learner needs instruction or corrective feedback to learn the correct form of such syntactic structures (Spada, Lightbown, & White, 2005; L. White, 1991).

In addition, as has been proposed by Pienemann (1984) (and discussed in Chapters 5 and 6), the acquisition of some grammatical structures may follow developmental sequences. That is, learners acquire these structures in a series of predetermined stages, such as the English question formations. Such structures may be learned more successfully if instruction accords with learners' developmental readiness (e.g., Mackey & Philp, 1998; Spada & Lightbown, 1993). Of course, as noted before, it may not be practically easy to tailor instruction to individual learners' developmental levels because it is hard to know whether or not certain learners are developmentally ready to learn a particular structure (see R. Ellis, 2005, 2006). However, this does not negate the value of instruction. Although teaching a particular target structure may not exactly accord with learners' developmental level, instruction can be very helpful if it targets features that are not too distant from learners' current level of language development (R. Ellis, 2005; Lightbown, 1998).

In Chapters 5 and 6, we briefly discussed the role of individual differences. We pointed out that learners are different individuals with different aptitude, personality characteristics, language proficiency, motivation, attitudes towards learning, and cultural backgrounds. The effects of instruction may also be mediated by these factors. For example, instruction may be more effective when the learner is highly motivated to learn than when he or she is not (see, for example, Dornyei, 2006; Dornyei & Skehan, 2003).

Point 2: Successful Instruction is Multifaceted

Much has been written these days about curriculum and syllabus designs, reflecting the general view that curriculum should be multidimensional (Stern, 1992). Multidimensional curriculum contains components of both grammar instruction and communicative language usage, with the general goals of accuracy, fluency, and complexity (Skehan, 1996a, 1996b). It is clear that no one instructional strategy or method can address all the goal dimensions of language pedagogy. The attainment of different goals requires different instructional strategies, and the success of these strategies depends heavily on the nature and quality of instruction. In this book we have presented a number of instructional strategies that provide opportunities for learners to focus on form and meaning. Incorporating grammar into target language use and applying it to communicative practices, as presented in this book, allows for the development of both accuracy and fluency. However, developing communicative ability does not occur easily. Learners need to spend considerable time and effort to reach a stage where they can use language features they have encountered in classroom instruction correctly and fluently in spontaneous discourse (Lightbown, 2004). To this end, learners need sustained exposure to the target language input, ample opportunities for output, as well as systematic instruction and corrective feedback in order to develop the kind of accuracy, fluency, and complexity they need in a given language.

In addition, communicative competence involves pragmatic competence (the ability to interpret and use utterances appropriately in social context). Therefore, grammar instruction needs to be supported by the provision of ample opportunities for interpreting and producing authentic discourse both inside and outside the classroom (see Chapter 4). In the classroom, this can be achieved by using various kinds of communicative and problem-solving grammar tasks that provide opportunities for both guided as well as free practices (Chapter 6). Communicative tasks push learners to focus on meaning and also allow them to use their own linguistic resources to express their intended meaning (e.g., R. Ellis, 2003). However, learners also need to constantly revisit and recycle the grammatical structures they have encountered in their lessons to consolidate already known forms. They also need to continue their attempts beyond what they get from classroom instruction and make sustained efforts outside the classroom. To this end, they need a high degree of intrinsic motivation (i.e., personal motivation based on learners' needs and desire) as well as positive rewards towards success from the teacher in the classroom and from others outside (H. D. Brown, 2000). These factors ensure that learners become real and autonomous language learners.

Point 3: SLA Theory and Research can only Provide Proposals that can be Tested and Examined in Language Classrooms, not Final Solutions

As this book has noted throughout the chapters, it is critical that research should inform grammar teaching. We discussed a number of strategies derived from SLA theory and research about how to teach grammar communicatively. Such strategies offer a range of opportunities for grammar instruction implicitly, explicitly, and in a variety of contexts. However, we should keep in mind that SLA theory and research can only provide proposals that can be tested and examined in language classrooms, not final solutions to teaching problems. SLA theory or research can inform pedagogical practices, but they are not the only source, or even the primary source of information for teachers' decisions (Lightbown, 2000). They can enhance teachers' awareness of the way language learning and teaching take place and consequently may make them more intellectually engaged with the teaching and learning process (Larsen-Freeman, 1995). However, they cannot tell teachers what to do. Therefore, as Widdowson (1990) stressed, teachers should always examine the relevance of such ideas in their own classrooms.

Consistent with the above perspective, our intention in this book has not been to prescribe, but to provide ideas that teachers can try, and assess their potential relevance within their own classroom contexts. It is our hope that these ideas can serve as a guideline and as a source of insight for communicative teaching of grammar in the classroom.

Point 4: Teachers Should be Eclectic in their Instructional Approach

There have been many books written about curriculum and syllabus design over the past decade (see, for example, Celce-Murcia, 2001b; Cook & North, 2010; Hall & Hewings, 2001; Hinkel, 2005, among others) and the current view is that curriculum should contain components of grammar instruction, communicative language usage, writing skills, comprehension skills, listening skills and reading skills, often text- or genre-based. This combination should also include an emphasis on both understanding and producing the target language for both meaning and accuracy. This is especially true for teaching English, which has become the language of global communication.

In addition, in recent years, many researchers and L2 educators have argued that language pedagogy is now in the post-methods era, shifting focus from prescribing specific methods as a key to success of language pedagogy to examining the processes involved in learning and teaching (see, for example, Kumaravadivelu, 1994, 2006). Long (1991), for example, questioned the whole concept of method and argued that although books on methods are very popular, "it is no exaggeration to say that language teaching methods do not exist – at least, not where they would matter, if they did, in the classroom" (p. 39).

A corollary of the above points is that teachers should be eclectic in their pedagogical approach. That is, they should choose and synthesize the best elements, principles and activities of different approaches to grammar teaching to attain success. Thus, not only do teachers have to maximize opportunities for the students to encounter important target forms in communicative contexts, they also need to be flexible and use a variety of means to do so.

However, this does not imply that teachers should choose pedagogical tools and techniques in a random manner. To be effective, any combination of strategies needs to be conducted in a principled way. Of course, it might be difficult to know exactly which combination is most effective for a given context, due to the complexity of any teaching context and the multitude of factors that play a role in that context. Nevertheless, there may be preferred ways of combining form-focused and meaning-focused activities depending on the pedagogical aims of the program, the instructional style of the teacher, and the needs of both the curriculum and the learners.

As discussed in Chapter 8, for example, in some situations (such as in foreign language situations), teachers might prioritize an implicit form-focused instruction, combined with some explicit explanation in the target language as a support. The implicit instruction can take the form of frequent exposure to language forms in the input such as input flooding, or drawing learners' attention to form through textual enhancement. In other situations, however, (such as in second language situations), they may use a more explicit approach, involving more overt instruction or corrective feedback (such as metalinguistic feedback or comments). In general, the strong version of form-focused activities, with the target structure embedded in communicative activities, might be preferred by many second language teachers because learners would very likely receive reinforcement from target language use as it is naturally encountered outside the classroom. However, when the target structure is one that might be encountered less frequently, explicit instruction on the structure could be delivered with the focus of the lesson remaining on meaningful content. In both situations, grammar instruction can be delivered either integratively or sequentially, which are two different ways of incorporating form-focused instruction into communicative contexts (Spada & Lightbown, 2008). In the former, attention to form occurs while learners' primary focus is on meaning, whereas in the latter, instruction takes the forms of mini-lessons used either before or after communicative activities.

Point 5: Teachers are not Agents to Learn and Apply Methods, but Professional Decision-Makers

Related to the above point is that teachers are not agents who learn skills and then apply them to pedagogical contexts. Teachers are active decision-makers, who make their pedagogical choices by "drawing on complex practically-oriented, personalized, and context-sensitive networks of knowledge, thoughts and beliefs" (Borg, 2003, p. 81). This view is consistent with a cognitive view of teaching, and the idea that teachers have their own personal theories of language teaching consisting of technical knowledge of the subject matter and intuitive knowledge developed through "reflection in and on actions" (R. Ellis, 1997, p. 62).

Thus, the needs of the learners, the particular instructional context, and the aim of empowering learner autonomy must inform the teacher's choice in grammar instruction. Any informed decision should also be based on a good understanding of not only effective strategies but also the way they help second language development. However, as Borg (2003) has emphasized, successful teachers are reflective, constructing their own knowledge through an active process of thinking and exploring.

Final Remarks

In this chapter, we began with a summary of the key themes of the book and then offered a number of additional remarks regarding grammar instruction and its implications for second language development. These remarks were related to the complexity of learning and teaching grammar, the relationship between SLA research and language teaching, and the appreciation of the role of teachers as strategic decision-makers. We also pointed out that teachers should be eclectic and select from a repertoire of instructional strategies to address the unique needs and goals of their learners and contexts. We would like to end this chapter by emphasizing this last point highly.

In this book we have presented a number of theoretically and empirically motivated instructional strategies that provide opportunities for learners to focus on form and meaning. However, we also stated that SLA theory and research offer general guidelines or, at best, ideas whose relevance should be tried out in classroom contexts. Furthermore, it should not be assumed that if researchers find that something is effective for language teaching, L2 teachers can use it in their L2 classrooms (R. Ellis, 1997). So how can teachers use the ideas and insights from research to offer their students the kind of learning opportunities they need in their own specific contexts?

As an old saying goes, experience is the best teacher. This is especially true when it comes to language teaching. Through experience, the interface between theory and practice becomes evident, and a better understanding of one's teaching practice develops. As teachers work with combinations of various instructional options, they develop a vision of what works and what does not work for them as well as how to amend or modify practice to increase their effectiveness. As teachers do so, they also recognize that many instructional options have common features. This will help them develop an appreciation for an eclectic vision and to choose and integrate a multitude of instructional options suitable for their own particular classroom situation.

Bibliography

Alanen, R. (1995). Input enhancement and rule presentation in second language acquisition. In R. Schmidt (Ed.), *Attention and awareness in foreign language acquisition* (pp. 259–302). Honolulu: University of Hawaii Press.

Aljaafreh, A., & Lantolf, J. (1994). Negative feedback as regulation and second language learning in the zone of proximal development. *Modern Language Journal, 78*, 465–83.

Allen, L. Q. (2000). Form-meaning connections and the French causative: An experiment in processing instruction. *Studies in Second Language Acquisition, 22*, 69–84.

Altarriba, J., & Heredia, R. (Eds.) (2008). *An introduction to bilingualism: Principles and processes.* Mahwah, NJ: Lawrence Erlbaum Associates.

Ammar, A., & Spada, N. (2006). One size fits all? Recasts, prompts, and L2 learning. *Studies in Second Language Acquisition, 28*, 543–74.

Anderson, J. C. (1982). Acquisition of cognitive skill. *Psychological Review, 89*, 369–406.

——(1983). *The architecture of cognition.* Cambridge, MA: Harvard University Press.

Appel, G., & Lantolf, J. (1994). *Vygotskian approaches to second language research.* Norwood, NJ: Ablex Pub. Corp.

Austin, J. L. (1962). *How to do things with words.* Cambridge, MA: Harvard University Press.

Ausubel, D., Novak, J., & Hanesian, H. (Eds.). (1978). *Educational psychology* (2nd ed.). New York: Holt, Rinehart & Winston.

Azar, B. S. (2003). *Fundamentals of English grammar* (3rd ed.). White Plains, NY: Pearson.

Bachman, L. (1990). *Fundamental considerations in language testing.* Oxford: Oxford University Press.

Baker, C. (2000). *A parents' and teachers' guide to bilingualism.* Clevedon: Multilingual Matters.

——(2006). *Foundations of bilingual education and bilingualism* (4th ed.). Clevedon: Multilingual Matters.

Batstone, R. (1994). *Grammar.* Oxford: Oxford University Press.

——(2002). Contexts of engagement: A discourse perspective on 'intake' and 'pushed output.' *System, 30*, 1–14.

Batstone, R., & Ellis, R. (2009). Principled grammar teaching. *System, 37*, 194–204.

Bell, A. (2008). Interactional feedback and ESL question development. Unpublished MA thesis, University of Victoria, Victoria, BC.

Beardsmore, B. (1993). The European School Model. In B. Beardsmore (Ed.), *European Models of Bilingual Education* (pp. 121–54). Clevedon: Multilingual Matters.

Benati, A. (2001). A comparative study of the effects of processing instruction and output-based instruction on the acquisition of the Italian future tense. *Language Teaching Research, 5*, 95–127.

——(2004). The effects of structured input activities and explicit information on the acquisition of the Italian future tense. In B. VanPatten (Ed.), *Processing instruction: Theory, research, and commentary* (pp. 207–25). Mahwah, NJ: Lawrence Erlbaum.

Benati, A., & Lee, J. (2008). *Grammar acquisition and processing instruction: Secondary and cumulative effects*. Clevedon: Multilingual Matters.

Bernardini, S. (2004). Corpora in the classroom: An overview and some reflections on future developments. In J. Sinclair (Ed.), *How to use corpora in language teaching* (pp. 15–36). Amsterdam: John Benjamins.

Berry, R. (2004). Awareness of metalanguage. *Language Awareness, 13*, 1–16.

Biber, D., Conrad, S., & Reppen, R. (1998). *Corpus linguistics: Investigating language and use*. Cambridge: Cambridge University Press.

Biber, D., Johansson, G., Leech, S., Conrad, S., & Finegan, E. (1999). *Longman grammar of spoken and written English*. Harlow: Pearson Education.

Biber, D., & Reppen, R. (2002). What does frequency have to do with grammar teaching? *Studies in Second Language Acquisition, 24*, 199–208.

Borg, S. (2003). Teacher cognition in language teaching: A review of research on what language teachers think, know, believe, and do. *Language Teaching, 36*, 81–109.

Braidi, S. M. (2002). Reexamining the role of recasts in native-speaker/nonnative-speaker interactions. *Language Learning, 52*, 1–42.

Braine, G. (2010). *Nonnative speaker English teachers: Research, pedagogy and professional growth*. Mahwah, NJ: Lawrence Erlbaum Associates.

Breen, M. P. (1984). Process syllabuses for the language classroom. In C. Brumfit (Ed.), *General English syllabus design. (ELT documents no. 118)* (pp. 47–60). London: Pergamon Press & The British Council.

Breen, M. P., & Candlin, C. (1980). The essentials of a communicative curriculum in language teaching. *Applied Linguistics, 1*, 89–112.

Brown, G., & Yule, G. (1994). *Teaching the spoken language*. New York: Cambridge University Press.

Brown, H. D. (2000). *Principles of language learning and teaching* (4th ed.). White Plains, NY: Longman.

Brown, J. D., & Kondo-Brown, K. (Eds.). (2006). *Perspectives on teaching connected speech to second language speakers*. Honolulu, HI: University of Hawaii Press.

Brown, K. (2001). World Englishes in TESOL programs: An infusion model of curricular innovation. In D. Hall, & A. Hewings (Eds.), *Innovation in English language teaching* (pp. 108–17). New York: Routledge.

Brown, R., & Hanlon, C. (1970). Derivational complexity and order of acquisition in child speech. In J. Hayes (Ed.), *Cognition and the development of language* (pp. 11–53). New York: John Wiley.

Bruce, I. (2008). *Academic writing and genre: A systematic analysis*. London: Continuum.

Brumfit, C. (1984). *Communicative methodology in language teaching: The roles of fluency and accuracy*. Cambridge: Cambridge University Press.

Burns, A., & Coffin, C. (Eds.). (2003). *Analysing English in a global context: A reader*. Macquarie: The Open University.

Burt, M. K., & Kiparsky, C. (1974). Global and local mistakes. In J. Schumann, & N. Stenson (Eds.), *New frontiers in second language learning* (pp. 71–80). Rowley, MA: Newbury House.

Butler, C. (2003). *Structure and function: A guide to three major structural-functional theories part 2: From clause to discourse and beyond*. Philadelphia, PA: John Benjamins.

Bygate, M., Skehan, P., & Swain, M. (Eds.). (2001). *Researching pedagogic tasks: Second language learning, teaching and testing*. New York: Longman.

Cadierno, T. (1995). Formal instruction from a processing perspective: An investigation into the Spanish past tense. *Modern Language Journal, 79*, 179–93.

Cameron, B. (2007). *Opportunities in teaching English to speakers of other languages*. New York: McGraw-Hill.

Canale, M., & Swain, M. (1980). Theoretical bases of communicative approaches to language teaching and testing. *Applied Linguistics, 1*, 1–47.

Carroll, S., & Swain, M. (1993). Explicit and implicit negative feedback: An empirical study of the learning of linguistic generalizations. *Studies in Second Language Acquisition, 15*, 357–86.

Celce-Murcia, M. (1991). *Teaching English as a second or foreign language* (2nd ed.). Boston: Newbury House.

——(2001a). Language teaching approaches: An overview. In M. Celce-Murcia (Ed.), *Teaching English as a second or foreign language* (pp. 3–11). Boston: Heinle & Heinle.

——(2001b). *Teaching English as a second or foreign language* (3rd ed.). Boston: Heinle & Heinle.

——(2002). Why it makes sense to teach grammar in context and through discourse. In E. Hinkel, & S. Fotos (Eds.), *New perspectives on grammar teaching in second language classrooms*. Mahwah, NJ: Lawrence Erlbaum Associates.

Celce-Murcia, M., & Hilles, S. (1988). *Techniques and resources in teaching grammar*. New York: Oxford University Press.

Celce-Murcia, M., & Larsen-Freeman, D. (2003). *The grammar book: An ESL/EFL teacher's course*. Boston: Heinle & Heinle.

Celce-Murcia, M., & Olshtain, E. (2001). *Discourse and context in language teaching: A guide for language teachers*. Cambridge: Cambridge University Press.

Chastain, K. (1981). Native speaker evaluation of student composition errors. *Modern Language Journal, 65*, 288–94.

Chaudron, C. (1977). A descriptive model of discourse in the corrective treatment of learners' errors. *Language Learning, 27*, 29–46.

Cheng, A. (2002). The effects of processing instruction on the acquisition of ser and estar. *Hispania, 85*, 900–09.

Chomsky, N. (1965). *Aspects of the theory of syntax*. Cambridge, MA: MIT Press.

Colina, A., & García Mayo, M. (2009). Oral interaction in task-based EFL learning: The use of the L1 as a cognitive tool. *International Review of Applied Linguistics, 47*, 325–45.

Cook, G., & North, S. (Eds.). (2010). *Applied linguistics in action: A reader*. New York: Routledge.

Corder, S. P. (1967). The significance of learners' errors. *International Review of Applied Linguistics, 5*, 161–69.

——(1977). Language teaching and learning: A social enounter. In H. Brown, C. Yorio & C. R. (Eds.), *On TESOL '77* (pp. 21–33). Washington, DC: TESOL.

Crookes, G., & Chaudron, C. (2001). Guidelines for language classroom instruction. In M. Celce-Murcia (Ed.), *Teaching English as a second or foreign language* (pp. 29–42). Boston: Heinle & Heinle.

Crookes, G., & Gass, S. (Eds.). (1993a). *Tasks and language learning: Integrating theory and practice*. Clevedon: Multilingual Matters.

——(1993b). *Tasks in a pedagogical context: Integrating theory and practice*. Clevedon: Multilingual Matters.

Crystal, D. (1980). *A first dictionary of linguistics and phonetics*. London: Deutsch.

——(1992). *Introducing linguistics*. London: Penguin.

Day, R., & Bamford, J. (1998). *Extensive reading in the second language classroom*. Cambridge: Cambridge University Press.

de Bot, K. (1996). The psycholinguistics of the output hypothesis. *Language Learning*, 46, 529–55.

DeKeyser, R. (1998). Beyond focus on form. In C. Doughty, & J. Williams (Eds.), *Focus on form in classroom language acquisition* (pp. 42–63). Cambridge: Cambridge University Press.

DeKeyser, R., & Juffs, A. (2005). Cognitive considerations in L2 learning. In E. Hinkel (Ed.), *Handbook of research in second language teaching and learning* (pp. 437–54). Mahwah, NJ: Lawrence Erlbaum Associates.

DeKeyser, R., Salaberry, R., Robinson, P., & Harrington, M. (2002). What gets processed in processing instruction? A commentary on Bill VanPatten's 'Processing instruction: An update'. *Language Learning*, 52, 805–23.

de la Campa, J., & Nassaji, H. (2009). The amount, purpose, and reasons for using L1 in L2 classrooms. *Foreign Language Annals*, 4, 742–59.

Demetras, M., Post, K., & Snow, C. (1986). Feedback to first language learners: The role of repetitions and clarification questions. *Child Language*, 13, 275–92.

Dickins, P., & Woods, E. (1988). Some criteria for the development of communicative language tasks. *TESOL Quarterly*, 22, 623–46.

DiPietro, R. (1987). *Strategic interaction: Learning language through scenarios*. Cambridge: Cambridge University Press.

Donato, R. (1994). Collective scaffolding in second language learning. In J. Lantolf, & G. Appel (Eds.), *Vygotskian approaches to second language research* (pp. 33–59). Norwood, NJ: Ablex.

Dornyei, Z. (2006). Individual differences in second language acquisition. *ILA Review*, 19, 42–68.

Dornyei, Z., & Skehan, P. (2003). Individual differences in second language learning. In D. C. Long, & M. Long (Eds.), *The handbook of second language acquisition* (pp. 589–630). Oxford: Blackwell.

Doughty, C. (1994). Fine-tuning of feedback by competent speakers to language learners. In J. Alatis (Ed.), *Georgetown University round table 1993: Strategic interaction and language acquisition* (pp. 96–108). Washington, DC: Georgetown University Press.

——(2001). Cognitive underpinning of focus on form. In P. Robinson (Ed.), *Cognition and second language instruction* (pp. 206–57). Cambridge: Cambridge University Press.

——(2003). Instructed SLA: Constraints, compensation, and enhancement In C. J. Doughty, & M. H. Long (Eds.), *The handbook of second language acquisition* (pp. 256–310). Oxford: Blackwell.

Doughty, C., & Long, M. (2003). Optimal psycholinguistic environments for distance foreign language learning. *Language Learning & Technology*, 7, 50–80.

Doughty, C., & Pica, T. (1986). Information gap tasks: Do they facilitate second language-acquisition? *TESOL Quarterly*, 20, 305–25.

Doughty, C., & Varela, E. (1998). Communicative focus on form. In C. Doughty, & J. Williams (Eds.), *Focus on form in classroom second language acquisition* (pp. 114–38). Cambridge: Cambridge University Press.

Doughty, C., & Williams, J. (1998). Pedagogical choices in focus on form. In C. Doughty, & J. Williams (Eds.), *Focus on form in classroom second language acquisition* (pp. 197–261). Cambridge: Cambridge University Press.

Edlund, J. (1995). The rainbow and the stream: Grammar as system versus language in use. In S. Hunter, & R. Wallace (Eds.), *The place of grammar in writing instruction: past, present and future* (pp. 204–13). Portsmouth, NH: Heinemann.

Ellis, N. (1995). Consciousness in second language acquisition: A review of field studies and laboratory experiments. *Language Awareness, 4,* 123–146.

——(2002). Frequency effects in language processing: A review with implications for theories of implicit and explicit language acquisition. *Studies in Second Language Acquisition, 24,* 143–88.

——(2007). The weak interface, consciousness and form-focused instruction: Mind the doors. In S. Fotos, & H. Nassaji (Eds.), *Form-focused instruction and teacher education: Studies in honour of Rod Ellis* (pp. 117–134). Oxford: Oxford University Press.

Ellis, N., & Schmidt, R. (1998). Rules or associations in the acquisition of morphology? The frequency by regularity interaction in human and PDP learning of morphosyntax. *Language and Cognitive Processes, 13,* 307–36.

Ellis, R. (1982). Informal and formal approaches to communicative language teaching. *ELT Journal, 36,* 73–81.

——(1993a). Interpretation-based grammar teaching. *System, 21,* 69–78.

——(1993b). Talking shop: Second language acquisition research: How does it help teachers? *ELT Journal, 47,* 3.

——(1994). *The study of second language acquisition.* Oxford: Oxford University Press.

——(1995). Interpretation tasks for grammar teaching. *TESOL Quarterly, 29,* 87–105.

——(1997). *SLA research and language teaching.* Oxford: Oxford University Press.

——(1999). Input-based approaches to teaching grammar: A review of classroom-oriented research. *Annual Review of Applied Linguistics, 19,* 64–80.

——(2001a). *Form-focused instruction and second language learning.* Malden, MA: Blackwell Publishers.

——(2001b). Introduction: Investigating form-focused instruction. *Language Learning, 51,* 1–46.

——(2002). Grammar teaching—practice or consciousness-raising? In J. C. Richards, & W. A. Renandya (Eds.), *Methodology in language teaching: An anthology of current practice* (pp. 167–74). Cambridge: Cambridge University Press.

——(2003). *Task-based language learning and teaching.* Oxford: Oxford University Press.

——(2005). Principles of instructed language learning. *System, 33,* 209–24.

——(2006). Current issues in the teaching of grammar: An SLA perspective. *TESOL Quarterly, 40,* 83–107.

——(2008). *The study of second language acquisition* (2nd ed.). Oxford: Oxford University Press.

——(2009). Corrective feedback and teacher development. *L2 Journal, 1,* 3–18.

Ellis, R., Basturkmen, H., & Loewen, S. (2001). Learner uptake in communicative ESL lessons. *Language Learning, 51,* 281–318.

——(2002). Doing focus-on-form. *System, 30,* 419–32.

Ellis, R., & Fotos, S. (Eds.). (1999). *Learning a second language through interaction.* Philadelphia, PA: John Benjamins.

Ellis, R., & Gaies, S. (1999). *Impact grammar: Grammar through listening.* Hong Kong: Addison-Wesley Longman.

Ellis, R., Loewen, S., & Erlam, R. (2006). Implicit and explicit corrective feedback and the acquisition of L2 grammar. *Studies in Second Language Acquisition, 28,* 339–69.

Ellis, R., & Sheen, Y. (2006). Reexamining the role of recasts in second language acquisition. *Studies in Second Language Acquisition, 28,* 575–600.

Ellis, R., Tanaka, Y., & Yamazaki, A. (1994). Classroom interaction, comprehension, and the acquisition of L2 word meanings. *Language Learning, 44,* 449–91.

Erlam, R. (2003). Evaluating the relative effectiveness of structured-input and output-based instruction in foreign language learning. *Studies in Second Language Acquisition, 25,* 559–82.

Farley, A. P. (2001). Authentic processing instruction and the Spanish subjunctive. *Hispania, 84,* 289–99.

——(2005). *Structured input: Grammar instruction for the acquisition-oriented classroom.* New York: McGraw-Hill.

Farrar, M. J. (1990). Discourse and the acquisition of grammatical morphemes. *Journal of Child Language, 17,* 607–24.

——(1992). Negative evidence and grammatical morpheme acquisition. *Developmental Psychology, 28,* 90–98.

Finocchiaro, M. B., & Brumfit, C. (1983). *The functional-notional approach: From theory to practice.* New York: Oxford University Press.

Firth, J. R. (1957). *Paper in linguistics.* London: Oxford University Press.

Flynn, S. (1996). A parameter-setting approach to second language acquisition. In W. Ritchie, & T. Bhatia (Eds.), *Handbook of second language acquisition* (pp. 121–58). San Diego: Academic Press.

Fortune, A. (2005). Learners' use of metalanguage in collaborative form-focused L2 output tasks. *Language Awareness, 14,* 21–37.

Fotos, S. (1993). Consciousness-raising and noticing through focus on form – grammar task-performance versus formal instruction. *Applied Linguistics, 14,* 385–407.

——(1994). Integrating grammar instruction and communicative language use through grammar consciousness-raising tasks. *TESOL Quarterly, 28,* 323–51.

——(1995). Problem-solving tasks for teaching If-Conditionals. In M. Pennington (Ed.) *New ways in teaching grammar* (pp. 83–87). Alexandria, VA: TESOL.

——(1998). Shifting the focus from forms to form in the EFL classroom. *ELT Journal, 52,* 301–7.

——(2002). Structure-based interactive tasks for the EFL grammar learner. In E. Hinkel, & S. Fotos (Eds.), *New perspectives on grammar teaching in second language classrooms* (pp. 135–54). Mahwah, NJ: Lawrence Erlbaum Associates.

——(2004). Writing as talking: E-mail exchange for promoting proficiency and motivation in the EFL classroom. In S. Fotos, & C. Browne (Eds.), *New perspectives on call for second language classrooms* (pp. 109–30). Mahwah, NJ: Lawrence Erlbaum Associates.

——(2005). Traditional and grammar translation methods for second language teaching. In E. Hinkel (Ed.), *Handbook of research in second language teaching and learning* (pp. 653–70). Mahwah, NJ: Lawrence Erlbaum Associates.

Fotos, S., & Browne, C. (2004). *New perspectives on call for second language classrooms.* Mahwah, NJ: Lawrence Erlbaum Associates.

Fotos, S., & Ellis, R. (1991). Communicating about grammar: A task-based approach. *TESOL Quarterly, 25,* 605–28.

Fotos, S., & Hinkel, E. (2007). Form-focused instruction and output for second language writing gains. In S. Fotos, & H. Nassaji (Eds.), *Form-focused instruction and teacher education: Studies in honour of Rod Ellis*. Oxford: Oxford University Press.

Fotos, S., Homan, R., & Poel, C. (1994). *Grammar in mind: Communicative English for fluency and accuracy*. Tokyo: Logos International.

Fotos, S., & Nassaji, H. (Eds.). (2007). *Form focused instruction and teacher education: Studies in honour of Rod Ellis*. Oxford: Oxford University Press.

García Mayo, M. P. (2002). Interaction in advanced EFL pedagogy: A comparison of form-focused activities. *International Journal of Educational Research, 37*, 323–41.

——(Ed.). (2007). *Investigating tasks in formal language learning* (Vol. 54). Clevedon: Multilingual Matters.

Gascoigne, C. (Ed.) (2007). *Assessing the impact of input enhancement in second language education*. Stillwater, OK: New Forums Press.

Gass, S. (1997). *Input, interaction, and the second language learner*. Mahwah, NJ: Lawrence Erlbaum.

——(2003). Input and interaction. In C. Doughty, & M. Long (Eds.), *The handbook of second language acquisition* (pp. 224–55). Oxford: Blackwell.

Gass, S., Mackey, A., & Pica, T. (1998). The role of input and interaction in second language acquisition: introduction to the special issue. *Modern Language Journal, 82*, 299–307.

Gass, S., & Selinker, L. (2008). *Second language acquisition: An introductory course*. (3rd ed.). New York: Taylor & Francis.

Gass, S., & Varonis, E. (1994). Input, interaction, and second language production. *Studies in Second Language Acquisition, 16*, 283–302.

Gee, J. P. (1999). *An introduction to discourse analysis: Theory and method*. New York: Routledge.

Godwin-Jones, B. (2001). Tools and trends in corpora use for teaching and learning. *Language Learning & Technology, 5*, 7–12.

Graddol, D. (1999). The decline of the native speaker. In D. Graddol, & U. Meinhof (Eds.), *English in a changing world. AILA review, 13* (pp. 57–68). Oxford: The English Company.

Grander, S., & Tribble, C. (1998). Learner corpus data in the foreign language classroom: Form focused instruction and data driven learning. In S. Granger (Ed.), *Learner English on computer* (pp. 199–209). London: Longman/Pearson.

Gumperz, J. J., & Hymes, D. H. (1972). *Directions in sociolinguistics: The ethnography of communication*. New York: Holt Rinehart and Winston.

Hall, D., & Hewings, A. (Eds.). (2001). *Innovation in teaching language: A reader*. London: Routledge.

Halliday, M. (1978). *Language as social semiotic: The social interpretation of language and meaning*. London: E. Arnold.

——(1984). Language as code and language as behavior: A systemic functional interpretation of the nature and ontogenesis of language. In R. Fawcett, M. A. K. Halliday, S. M. Lamb, & A. Makkai (Eds.), *The semiotics of culture and language* (Vol. 1). London: Frances Pinter.

——(1994). *An introduction to functional grammar* (2nd ed.). London: Edward Arnold.

——(2004). *An introduction to functional grammar* (3rd ed.). London: Hodder Arnold.

Halliday, M., & Matthiessen, C. (2004). *An introduction to functional grammar* (3rd ed.). London: Hodder Arnold.

Han, Z., Park, E., & Combs, C. (2008). Textual enhancement of input: Issues and possibilities. *Applied Linguistics, 29*, 597–618.

Harklau, L. (1994). ESL versus mainstream classes: Contrasting L2 learning environments. *TESOL Quarterly, 28*, 241–72.

Harley, B., & Swain, M. (1984). The interlanguage of immersion students and its implications for second language teaching. In A. Davies, C. Criper, & A. P. R. Howatt (Eds.), *Interlanguage* (pp. 291–311). Edinburgh: Edinburgh University Press.

Harmer, J. (1996). Is PPP dead? *Modern English Teacher, 5*, 7–14.

Hawkes, L. (2007). Recasts revisited: The role of recasts in error detection and correction by adult ESL students. Unpublished MA, University of Victoria, Victoria, BC.

Heaton, J., & Turton, N. (1987). *Longman dictionary of common errors*. New York: Longman.

Hendrickson, J. (1978). Error correction in foreign language teaching: Recent theory, research, and practice. *Modern Language Journal, 62*, 387–98.

Hertel, T., & Sunderman, G. (2009). Student attitudes towards native and non-native language instructors. *Foreign Language Annals, 42*, 468–82.

Hewings, A., & Hewings, M. (2005). *Grammar and context: An advanced resource book*. London: Routledge.

Hinkel, E. (1999). *Culture in second language teaching and learning*. New York: Cambridge University Press.

——(2002). *Second language writers' text: Linguistic and rhetorical features*. Mahwah, NJ: Lawrence Erlbaum Associates.

——(2004). *Teaching academic ESL writing: Practical techniques in vocabulary and grammar*. Mahwah, NJ: Lawrence Erlbaum Associates.

——(Ed.). (2005). *Handbook of research in second language teaching and learning*. Mahwah, NJ: Lawrence Erlbaum Associates.

Holliday, A. (2001). Achieving cultural continuity in curriculum innovation. In D. Hall, & A. Hewings (Eds.), *Innovation in English language teaching: A reader* (pp. 171–77). New York: Routledge.

Howatt, A. (1984). *A history of English language teaching*. Oxford: Oxford University Press.

Hunston, S., & Gill, F. (1998). Verbs observed: A corpus-driven pedagogic grammar. *Applied Linguistics, 19*, 45–72.

Hymes, D. (1972). On communicative competence. In J. B. Pride, & J. Holmes (Eds.), *Sociolinguistics* (pp. 269–93). Harmondsworth: Penguin.

Iwashita, N. (2001). The effect of learner proficiency on interactional moves and modified output in nonnative–nonnative interaction in Japanese as a foreign language. *System, 29*, 267–87.

Izumi, S. (2002). Output, input enhancement and the noticing hypothesis: An experimental study on ESL relativization. *Studies in Second Language Acquisition, 24*, 541–77.

Izumi, S., & Bigelow, M. (2000). Does output promote noticing and second language acquisition? *TESOL Quarterly, 34*, 239–78.

Izumi, S., Bigelow, M., Fujiwara, M., & Fearnow, S. (1999). Testing the output hypothesis: Effects of output on noticing and second language acquisition. *Studies in Second Language Acquisition, 21*, 421–52.

Janicki, K. (1985). *The foreigner's language*. Oxford: Pergamon.

Jenkins, J. (2003). *World Englishes: A resource book for students*. London: Routledge.

——(2006). *World Englishes: A resource book for students*. (2nd ed.). London: Routledge.

Johns, T., & King, P. (Eds.). (1991). *Classroom concordancing.* Birmingham: University of Birmingham.

Jourdenais, R., Ota, M., Stauffer, S., Boyson, B., & Doughty, C. (1995). Does textual enhancement promote noticing? A think-aloud protocol analysis. In R. Schmidt (Ed.), *Attention and awareness in second language learning* (pp. 183–216): Technical Report No. 9. Honolulu: University of Hawaii, Second Language Teaching and Curriculum Center.

Kachru, B. (1992). *The other tongue: English across cultures.* Urbana, IL: University of Illinois Press.

Kachru, B., & Nelson, C. (2006). World Englishes. In S. McKay, & N. Hornberger (Eds.), *Sociolinguistics and language education.* Cambridge: Cambridge University Press.

Kasper, G., & Blum-Kulka, S. (2003). *Interlanguage pragmatics.* Oxford: Oxford University Press.

Kelly, L. G. (1969). *25 centuries of language teaching: An inquiry into the science, art, and development of language teaching methodology, 500 B.C.–1969.* Rowley, MA: Newbury House Publishers.

Kowal, M., & Swain, M. (1994). Using collaborative language production tasks to promote students' language awareness. *Language Awareness, 3,* 73–93.

Krashen, S. (1981). *Second language acquisition and second language learning.* Oxford: Oxford University Press.

——(1985). *The input hypothesis: Issues and implications.* Oxford: Pergamon Press.

——(1993). The effect of formal grammar teaching: Still peripheral. *TESOL Quarterly, 27,* 722–25.

——(2008). Language education: Past, present, and future. *RELC Journal, 39,* 178–87.

Krashen, S., & Terrell, T. (1983). *The natural approach: Language acquisition in the classroom.* Oxford: Pergamon.

Kumaravadivelu, B. (1994). The postmethod condition: (e)merging strategies for second/foreign language teaching. *TESOL Quarterly, 28,* 27–48.

——(2006). TESOL methods: Changing tracks, challenging trends. *TESOL Quarterly, 40,* 59–81.

Labov, W. (1972). *Sociolinguistic patterns.* Philadelphia, PA: University of Pennsylvania Press.

Lantolf, J. (2000). *Sociocultural theory and second language learning.* Oxford: Oxford University Press.

LaPierre, D. (1994). Language output in a cooperative learning setting: Determining its effects on second language learning. Unpublished MA thesis, OISE, University of Toronto, Toronto.

Lapkin, S., Hart, D., & Swain, M. (1991). Early and middle French immersion programs: French-language outcomes. *Canadian Modern Language Review, 48,* 11–40.

Lapkin, S., & Swain, M. (2000). Task outcomes: A focus on immersion students' use of pronominal verbs in their writing. *Canadian Journal of Applied Linguistics, 3,* 7–22.

——(2004). What underlies immersion students' production: The case of 'Avoir besoin de'. *Foreign Language Annals, 37,* 349–55.

Lapkin, S., Swain, M., & Shapson, S. (1990). French immersion research agenda for the 90s. *Canadian Modern Language Review, 46,* 638–74.

Lapkin, S., Swain, M., & Smith, M. (2002). Reformulation and the learning of French pronominal verbs in a Canadian French immersion context. *Modern Language Journal, 86,* 485–507.

Larsen-Freeman, D. (1995). On the teaching and learning of grammar: Challenging the myths. In F. Eckman, D. Highland, L. P. J. Mileham, & R. Weber (Eds.), *Second language acquisition theory and pedagogy* (pp. 131–50). Mahwah, NJ: Lawrence Erlbaum.

——(2001). Teaching grammar. In M. Celce-Murcia (Ed.), *Teaching English as a second or foreign language* (3rd ed., pp. 251–85). MA: Heinle & Heinle.

——(2003). *Teaching language: From grammar to grammarin.* Boston: Thomson Heinle.

Larsen-Freeman, D., & Long, M. H. (1991). *An introduction to second language acquisition research.* London: Longman.

Lazaraton, A. (2001). Teaching oral skills. In M. Celce-Murcia (Ed.), *Teaching English as a second or foreign language* (pp. 103–15). Boston: Heinle & Heinle.

Lee, J., & VanPatten, B. (2003). *Making communicative language teaching happen* (2nd ed.). Boston: McGraw-Hill.

Leech, G., & Svartvik, J. (2003). *A communicative grammar of English* (3rd ed.). New York: Pearson ESL.

Leeser, M. (2004). Learner proficiency and focus on form during collaborative dialogue. *Language Teaching Research, 8,* 55–81.

Levy, M. (1997). *Computer-assisted language learning: Context and conceptualization.* New York: Oxford University Press.

Li, D. (2001). Teachers' perceived difficulties in introducing the communicative approach in South Korea. In D. Hall, & A. Hewings (Eds.), *Innovation in English language teaching: A reader* (pp. 149–65). New York: Routledge.

Lightbown, P. (1992). What have we here? Some observations on the influence of instruction on L2 learning. In R. Philipson, E. Kellerman, L. Selinker, M. Sharwood Smith, & M. Swain (Eds.), *Foreign language pedagogy research: A commemorative volume for Claus Faerch* (pp. 197–212). Clevedon: Multilingual Matters.

——(1998). The importance of timing in focus on form. In C. Doughty, & J. Williams (Eds.), *Focus on form in classroom second language acquisition* (pp. 177–94). Cambridge: Cambridge University Press.

——(2000). Anniversary article: Classroom SLA research and second language teaching. *Applied Linguistics, 21,* 431–62.

——(2004). Commentary: What to teach? How to teach? In B. VanPatten (Ed.), *Processing instruction: Theory, research, and commentary* (pp. 65–78). Mahwah, NJ: Lawrence Erlbaum Associates.

Lightbown, P., & Spada, N. (1993). *How languages are learned.* Oxford: Oxford University Press.

——(1999). *How languages are learned* (2nd ed.). Oxford: Oxford University Press.

Liu, D., & Master, P. (Eds.). (2003). *Grammar teaching in teacher education.* Alexandria, VA: TESOL.

Lock, G. (1996). *Functional English grammar: An introduction for second language teachers.* New York: Cambridge University Press.

Loewen, S., & Nabei, T. (2007). Measuring the effects of oral corrective feedback on L2 knowledge. In A. Mackey (Ed.), *Conversational interaction in second language acquisition: A series of empirical studies* (pp. 361–78). Oxford: Oxford University Press.

Loewen, S., & Philp, J. (2006). Recasts in adults English L2 classrooms: Characteristics, explicitness, and effectiveness. *Modern Language Journal, 90,* 536–56.

Long, M. (1983). Native speaker/non-native speaker conversation and the negotiation of comprehensible input. *Applied Linguistics, 4,* 126–41.

——(1985). Input and second language acquisition theory. In S. Gass, & C. Madden (Eds.), *Input in second language acquisition* (pp. 377–93). Rowley, MA: Newbury House.

——(1991). Focus on form: A design feature in language teaching methodology. In K. DeBot, R. Ginsberge, & C. Kramsch (Eds.), *Foreign language research in cross-cultural perspective* (pp. 39–52). Amsterdam: John Benjamins.

——(1996). The role of the linguistic environment in second language acquisition. In W. Ritchie, & T. Bhatia (Eds.), *Handbook of second language acquisition* (pp. 413–68). San Diego: Academic Press.

——(2000). Focus on form in task-based language teaching. In R. D. Lambert, & E. Shohamy (Eds.), *Language policy and pedagogy: Essays in honor of A. Ronald Walton* (pp. 179–92). Philadelphia, PA: John Benjamins.

——(Ed.). (2006). *Problems in SLA*. Mahwah, NJ: Lawrence Erlbaum.

Long, M., & Crookes, G. (1992). Three approaches to task-based syllabus design. *TESOL Quarterly, 26*, 27–56.

Long, M., & Robinson, P. (1998). Focus on form: Theory, research and practice. In C. Doughty, & J. Williams (Eds.), *Focus on form in classroom language acquisition* (pp. 15–41). Cambridge: Cambridge University Press.

Loschky, L., & Bley-Vroman, R. (1993). Grammar and task based methodology. In G. Crookes, & S. M. Gass (Eds.), *Tasks and language learning: Integrating theory and practice* (pp. 123–67). Clevedon: Multilingual Matters.

Lyster, R. (1998). Recasts, repetition, and ambiguity in L2 classroom discourse. *Studies in Second Language Acquisition, 20*, 51–81.

——(2001). Negotiation of form, recasts, and explicit correction in relation to error types and learner repair in immersion classrooms. *Language Learning, 51*, 265–301.

——(2004). Differential effects of prompts and recasts in form-focused instruction. *Studies in Second Language Acquisition, 26*, 399–432.

——(2007). *Learning and teaching languages through content: A counterbalanced approach*. Philadelphia, PA: John Benjamins.

Lyster, R., & Ranta, L. (1997). Corrective feedback and learner uptake: Negotiation of form in communicative classrooms. *Studies in Second Language Acquisition, 19*, 37–66.

Mackey, A. (Ed.). (2007). *Conversational interaction in second language acquisition: A collection of empirical studies*. Oxford: Oxford University Press.

Mackey, A., & Gass, S. (Eds.). (2006). *Pushing the methodological boundaries in interaction research* (special issue). *Studies in second language acquisition* (Vol. 28).

Mackey, A., Oliver, R., & Leeman, J. (2003). Interactional input and the incorporation of feedback: An exploration of NS-NNS and NNS-NNS adult and child dyads. *Language Learning, 53*, 35–66.

Mackey, A., & Philp, J. (1998). Conversational interaction and second language development: Recasts, responses, and red herrings? *Modern Language Journal, 82*, 338–56.

Mackey, A., & Silver, R. (2005). Interactional tasks and English L2 learning by immigrant children in Singapore. *System, 33*, 239–60.

McCarthy, M. (1991). *Discourse analysis for language teachers*. Cambridge: Cambridge University Press.

McCarthy, M., & Carter, R. (2002). Ten criteria for a spoken grammar. In E. Hinkel, & S. Fotos (Eds.), *New perspectives on grammar teaching in second language classrooms* (pp. 51–75). Mahwah, NJ: Lawrence Erlbaum.

McEnery, T., Xiao, R., & Tono, Y. (2006). *Corpus-based language studies: An advanced resource book*. London: Routledge.

McKay, S. (2002). *Teaching English as an international language: Rethinking goals and approaches*. Oxford: Oxford University Press.

McLaughlin, B. (1990). Restructuring. *Applied Linguistics, 11*, 113–28.

McLeod, B., & McLaughlin, B. (1986). Restructuring or automaticity? Reading in a second language. *Language Learning, 36*, 109–23.

McNamara, T., Hill, K., & May, L. (2002). Discourse and assessment. *Annual Review of Applied Linguistics, 22*, 221–42.

Medgyes, P. (1992). Native or non-native: Who's worth more? *ELT Journal, 46*, 340–49.

Mindt, D. (2002). A corpus-based grammar for ELT. In B. Kettemann, & G. Marko (Eds.), *Teaching and learning by doing corpus analysis* (pp. 91–104). Amsterdam: Rodopi.

Mitchell, R., & Myles, F. (2004). *Second language learning theories* (2nd ed.). New York: Arnold.

Mizumoto, A., & Takeuchi, O. (2009). Examining the effectiveness of explicit instruction of vocabulary learning strategies with Japanese EFL students. *Language Teaching Research, 13*, 425–50.

Morgan-Short, K., & Bowden, H. W. (2006). Processing instruction and meaningful output-based instruction: Effects on second language development. *Studies in Second Language Acquisition, 28*, 31–65.

Murray, D. (2000). Protean communication: The language of computer-mediated communication. *TESOL Quarterly, 34*, 397–422.

Nabei, T. (1996). Dictogloss: Is it an effective language learning task? *Working Papers in Educational Linguistics, 12*, 59–74.

Nabei, T., & Swain, M. (2002). Learner awareness of recasts in classroom interaction: A case study of an adult EFL student's second language learning. *Language Awareness, 11*, 43–63.

Nassaji, H. (1999). Towards integrating form-focused instruction and communicative interaction in the second language classroom: Some pedagogical possibilities. *Canadian Modern Language Review, 55*, 385–402.

——(2007a). Elicitation and reformulation and their relationship with learner repair in dyadic interaction. *Language Learning, 57*, 511–48.

——(2007b). Focus on form through recasts in dyadic student–teacher intercton: A case for recast enhancement. In C. Gascoigne (Ed.), *Assessing the impact of input enhancement in second language education* (pp. 53–69). Stillwater, OK: New Forums Press.

——(2007c). Reactive focus on form through negotiation on learners' written errors. In S. Fotos, & H. Nassaji (Eds.), *Form-focused instruction and teacher education: Studies in honour of Rod Ellis* (pp. 117–29). Oxford: Oxford University Press.

——(2009). Effects of recasts and elicitations in dyadic interaction and the role of feedback explicitness. *Language Learning, 59*, 411–52.

——(2010). The occurance and effectiveness of spontaneous focus on form in adult ESL classrooms. *Canadian Modern Language Review*.

Nassaji, H., & Cumming, A. (2000). What's in a ZPD? A case study of a young ESL student and teacher interacting through dialogue journals. *Language Teaching Research, 4*, 95–121.

Nassaji, H., & Fotos, S. (2004). Current developments in research on the teaching of grammar. *Annual Review of Applied Linguistics, 24*, 126–45.

——(2007). Current issues in form-focused instruction. In S. Fotos, & H. Nassaji (Eds.), *Form-focused instruction and teacher education: Studies in honour of Rod Ellis* (pp. 7–15). Oxford: Oxford University Press.

Nassaji, H., & Swain, M. (2000). Vygotskian perspective on corrective feedback in L2: The effect of random versus negotiated help on the learning of English articles. *Language Awareness, 9*, 34–51.

Nassaji, H., & Tian, J. (2010). Collaborative and individual output tasks and their effects on learning English phrasal verbs. *Language Teaching Research, 14*, 397–419.

Nesselhauf, N. (2004). Learner corpora and their potential for language teaching. In J. Sinclair (Ed.), *How to use corpora in language teaching* (pp. 125–52). Amsterdam: John Benjamins.

Nicholas, H., Lightbown, P., & Spada, N. (2001). Recasts as feedback to language learners. *Language Learning, 51*, 719–58.

Nobuyoshi, J., & Ellis, R. (1993). Focused communication tasks and second language acquisition. *ELT Journal, 47*, 113–28.

Norris, J. M., & Ortega, L. (2001). Does type of instruction make a difference? Substantive findings from a meta-analytic review. *Language Learning, 51*, 157–213.

Nunan, D. (1989). *Designing tasks for the communicative classroom*. Cambridge: Cambridge University Press.

——(1998). Teaching grammar in context. *ELT Journal, 52*, 101–9.

——(2001). *Expressions: Meaningful English communication* (book 3). Singapore: Thomson Learning.

——(2004). *Task-based language teaching*. Cambridge: Cambridge University Press.

——(2006). Task-based language teaching in the Asia context: Defining 'task.' *Asian EFL Journal, 8*, 12–18.

Ohta, A. S. (2001). *Second language acquisition processes in the classroom: Learning Japanese*. Mahwah, NJ: Lawrence Erlbaum Associates Publishers.

Panova, I., & Lyster, R. (2002). Patterns of corrective feedback and uptake in an adult ESL classroom. *TESOL Quarterly, 36*, 573–95.

Partington, A. (1998). *Patterns and meanings: Using corpora for English language research and teaching*. Amsterdam: John Benjamins.

Philp, J. (2003). Constraints on 'noticing the gap': Nonnative speakers' noticing of recasts in NS-NNS interaction. *Studies in Second Language Acquisition, 25*, 99–126.

Pica, T. (1987). Second-language acquisition, social interaction, and the classroom. *Applied Linguistics, 8*, 3–21.

——(1988). Interlanguage adjustments as an outcome of NS-NNS negotiated interaction. *Language Learning, 38*, 45–73.

——(1991). Input as a theoretical and research construct: From Corder's original definition to current views. *IRAL, International Review of Applied Linguistics in Language Teaching, 29*, 185–96.

——(1992). The textual outcomes of native speaker-non-native speaker negotiation: What do they reveal about second language learning? In C. Kramsch, & S. McConnell-Ginet (Eds.), *Text and context* (pp. 198–237). Cambridge, MA: D.C. Heath.

——(1994). Research on negotiation: What does it reveal about second-language learning conditions, processes, and outcomes? *Language Learning, 44*, 493–527.

——(1996). Do second language learners need negotiation? *International Review of Applied Linguistics in Language Teaching, 34*, 1–21.

——(1998). Second language learning through interaction: Multiple perspectives. In V. Regan (Ed.), *Contemporary approaches to second language acquisition in social context* (pp. 9–31). Dublin: University College Dublin Press.

——(2002). Subject-matter content: How does it assist the interactional and linguistic needs of classroom language learners? *Modern Language Journal, 86*, 1–19.

Pica, T., Kanagy, R., & Falodun, J. (1993). Choosing and using communicative tasks for second language instruction. In S. Gass, & G. Crookes (Eds.), *Tasks and language learning: Integrating theory and practice* (pp. 9–34). Clevedon: Multilingual Matters.

Pica, T., Kang, H., & Sauro, S. (2006). Information gap tasks: Their multiple roles and contributions to interaction research methodology. *Studies in Second Language Acquisition, 28*, 301–38.

Pienemann, M. (1984). Psychological constraints on the teachability of languages. *Studies in Second Language Acquisition, 6*, 186–214.

——(1989). Is language teachable? Psycholinguistic experiments and hypotheses. *Applied Linguistics, 10*, 52–79.

——(1998). *Language processing and second language development: Processability theory*. Amsterdam: John Benjamins.

Polio, C. (2007). A history of input enhancement: Defining an evolving concept. In C. Gascoigne (Ed.), *Assessing the impact of input enhancement in second language education* (pp. 1–18). Stillwater, OK: New Forums Press.

Prabhu, N. S. (1984). Procedural syllabuses. In T. E. Read (Ed.), *Trends in language syllabus design* (pp. 272–80). Singapore: Singapore University Press/RELC.

——(1987). *Second language pedagogy*. Oxford: Oxford University Press.

Rao, Z. (2001). Bridging the gap between teaching and learning styles in East Asian contexts. *TESOL Journal, 11*, 5–11.

Richards, J. C. (2002). Accuracy and fluency revisited. In E. Hinkel, & S. Fotos (Eds.), *New perspectives on grammar teaching in second language classrooms* (pp. 35–50). Mahwah, NJ: Lawrence Erlbaum Associates.

——(2003). *New interchange: English for international communication*. Cambridge: Cambridge University Press.

Richards, J. C., & Rodgers, T. (1986). *Approaches and methods in language teaching: A description and analysis*. Cambridge: Cambridge University Press.

——(2001). *Approaches and methods in language teaching* (2nd ed.). Cambridge: Cambridge University Press.

Robinson, P. (1995). Attention, memory, and the noticing hypothesis. *Language Learning, 45*, 283–331.

——(1996). Learning simple and complex second language rules under implicit, incidental, rule-search, and instructed conditions. *Studies in Second Language Acquisition, 18*, 27–67.

—— (Ed.). (2001). *Cognition and second language instruction*. Cambridge: Cambridge University Press.

——(2007). Criteria for classifying and sequencing pedagogical tasks. In M. García Mayo (Ed.), *Investigating tasks in formal language learning* (pp. 2–27). Clevedon: Multilingual Matters.

Robinson, P., & Gilabert, R. (Eds.). (2007). Task complexity, the cognition hypothesis and second language instruction (special issue). *International Review of Applied Linguistics, 43*.

Rose, K., & Kasper, G. (2001). *Pragmatics in language teaching*. New York: Cambridge University Press.

Rutherford, W. (1987). *Second language grammar: Learning and teaching*. New York: Longman.

——(1988). Functions of grammar in a language-teaching syllabus. In W. Rutherford, & M. Sharwood Smith (Eds.), *Grammar and second language teaching* (pp. 231–49). New York: Newbury House.

Rutherford, W., & Sharwood Smith, M. (1985). Consciousness-raising and universal grammar. *Applied Linguistics, 6*, 274–82.

Samuda, V., & Bygate, M. (2008). *Tasks in second language learning*. London: Palgrave.

Savignon, S. (2001). Communicative language teaching for the twenty-first century. In M. Celce-Murcia (Ed.), *Teaching English as a second or foreign language* (3rd ed., pp. 13–28). MA: Heinle & Heinle.

——(2005). Communicative language teaching: Strategies and goals. In E. Hinkel (Ed.), *Handbook on research in second language teaching and learning* (pp. 635–51). Mahwah, NJ: Lawrence Erlbaum Associates.

Sawar, Z. (2001). Adapting individualization techniques for large classes. In D. Hall, & A. Hewings (Eds.), *Innovation in English language teaching: A reader* (pp. 127–36). New York: Routledge.

Saxton, M. (1997). The contrast theory of negative input. *Journal of Child Language, 24*, 139–61.

Schiffrin, D., Tannen, D., & Hamilton, H. (2001). *The handbook of discourse analysis*. Oxford: Blackwell.

Schmidt, R. (1990). The role of consciousness in second language learning. *Applied Linguistics, 11*, 129–58.

——(1993). Awareness and second language acquisition. *Annual Review of Applied Linguistics, 13*, 206–26.

——(1995). Consciousness and foreign language learning: A tutorial on the role of attention and awareness in language learning. In R. Schmidt (Ed.), *Attention and awareness in foreign language learning* (pp. 1–63). Honolulu, HI: University of Hawaii Press.

——(2001). Attention. In P. Robinson (Ed.), *Cognition and second language instruction* (pp. 3–32). Cambridge: Cambridge University Press.

Schwartz, B. (1993). On explicit and negative data effecting and affecting competence and linguistic behavior. *Studies in Second Language Acquisition, 15*, 147–63.

Scott, M., & Tribble, C. (2006). *Textual patterns and corpus analysis in language education*. Amsterdam: John Benjamins.

Scrivener, J. (1996). ARC: A descriptive model for classroom work on language. In J. Willis, & D. Willis (Eds.), *Challenge and change in language teaching* (pp. 79–92). Oxford: Heinemann.

Searle, J. R. (1969). *Speech acts: An essay in the philosophy of language*. Cambridge: Cambridge University Press.

Sharwood Smith, M. (1981). Consciousness-raising and second language acquisition theory. *Applied Linguistics, 2*, 159–68.

——(1991). Speaking to many minds: On the relevance of different types of language information for the L2 learner. *Second Language Research, 72*, 118–32.

——(1993). Input enhancement in instructed SLA: Theoretical bases. *Studies in Second Language Acquisition, 15*, 165–79.

Sheen, R. (2007). Processing instruction. *ELT Journal, 61*, 161–63.

Sheen, Y. (2004). Corrective feedback and learner uptake in communicative classrooms across instructional settings. *Language Teaching Research, 8*, 263–300.

——(2008). Recasts, language anxiety, modified output, and L2 learning. *Language Learning, 58,* 835–74.

Shiffrin, R., & Schneider, W. (1977). Controlled and automatic human information processing: Perceptual learning, automatic, attending and a general theory. *Psychological Review, 84,* 127–90.

Simard, D. (2009). Differential effects of textual enhancement formats on intake. *System, 37,* 124–35.

Sinclair, J. (Ed.). (2004.). *How to use corpora in language teaching.* Amsterdam: John Benjamins.

Skehan, P. (1996a). A framework for the implementation of task-based instruction. *Applied Linguistics, 17,* 38–62.

——(1996b). Second language acquisition research and task-based instruction. In J. Willis, & D. Willis (Eds.), *Challenge and change in language teaching* (pp. 17–30). Oxford: Heinemann.

——(1998a). *A cognitive approach to language learning.* Oxford: Oxford University Press.

——(1998b). Task-based instruction. *Annual Review of Applied Linguistics, 18,* 268–86.

Snow, M. A. (2001). Content-based and immersion models for second and foreign langauge teaching. In M. Celce-Murcia (Ed.), *Teaching English as a second or foreign language* (pp. 303–32). Boston: Heinle & Heinle.

Snow, M. A., Met, M., & Genesee, F. (1992). A conceptual framework for the integration of language and content instruction. In P. A. Richard-Amato, & M. A. Snow (Eds.), *The multicultural classroom: Readings for content-area teachers* (pp. 27–38). Reading, MA: Addison-Wesley.

Spada, N. (1997). Form-focused instruction and second language acquisition: A review of classroom and laboratory research. *Language Teaching, 29,* 1–15.

Spada, N., & Lightbown, P. (1993). Instruction and the development of questions in L2 classrooms. *Studies in Second Language Acquisition, 15,* 205–24.

——(2008). Form-focused instruction: Isolated or integrated? *TESOL Quarterly, 42,* 181–120.

Spada, N., Lightbown, P., & White, J. (2005). The importance of form/meaning mappings in explicit form-focused instruction. *Investigations in Instructed Second Language Acquisition, 4,* 171–206.

Stern, H. (1992). *Issues and options in language teaching.* Oxford: Oxford University Press.

Storch, N. (1997). The editing talk of adult ESL learners. *Language Awareness, 6,* 221–32.

——(1998). A classroom-based study: Insights from a collaborative text reconstruction task. *ELT Journal, 52,* 291–300.

——(2001). How collaborative is pair work? ESL tertiary students composing in pairs. *Language Teaching Research, 5,* 29–53.

——(2007). Investigating the merits of pair work on a text editing task in ESL classes. *Language Teaching Research, 2,* 143–59.

Swain, M. (1985). Communicative competence: Some rules of comprehensible input and comprehensible output in its development. In S. Gass, & C. Madden (Eds.), *Input in second language acquisition* (pp. 235–53). Rowley, MA: Newbury House.

——(1993). The output hypothesis: Just speaking and writing aren't enough. *Canadian Modern Language Review, 50,* 158–64.

——(1995). Three functions of output in second language learning. In H. G. Widdowson, G. Cook, & B. Seidlhofer (Eds.), *Principle and practice in applied linguistics: Studies in honour of H. G. Widdowson* (pp. 125–44). Oxford: Oxford University Press.

——(1997). Collaborative dialogue: Its contribution to second language learning. *Revista Canaria de Estudios Ingleses, 34*, 115–32.

——(1998). Focus on form through conscious reflection. In C. Doughty, & J. Williams (Eds.), *Focus on form in classroom second language acquisition* (pp. 64–81). Cambridge: Cambridge University Press.

——(2005). The output hypothesis: Theory and research. In E. Hinkel (Ed.), *Handbook on research in second language teaching and learning* (pp. 471–83). Mahwah, NJ: Lawrence Erlbaum Associates.

Swain, M., & Lapkin, S. (1995). Problems in output and the cognitive-processes they generate: A step towards 2nd language-learning. *Applied Linguistics, 16*, 371–91.

——(1998). Interaction and second language learning: Two adolescent French immersion students working together. *Modern Language Journal, 82*, 320–37.

——(2001). Focus on form through collaborative dialogue: Exploring task effects. In M. Bygate, P. Skehan, & M. Swain (Eds.), *Researching pedagogic tasks: Second language learning, teaching and assessment*. London: Pearson International.

Swain, M., Lapkin, S., Knouzi, I., Suzuki, W., & Brooks, L. (2009). Languaging: Students learn the grammatical concept of voice in French. *Modern Language Journal, 93*, 5–29.

Thornbury, S. (1999). *How to teach grammar*. Harlow: Pearson Education.

——(2005). *Beyond the sentence: Introducing discourse analysis*. Oxford: Macmillan Publishers.

——(2006). *Grammar*. Oxford: Oxford University Press.

Tomlin, R. (1994). Functional grammars, pedagogical grammars and communicative language teaching. In T. Odlin (Ed.), *Perspectives on pedagogical grammar* (pp. 140–78). Cambridge: Cambridge University Press.

Tomlin, R., & Villa, V. (1994). Attention in cognitive science and second language acquisition. *Studies in Second Language Acquisition, 16*, 183–202.

Toth, P. D. (2006). Processing instruction and a role for output in second language acquisition. *Language Learning, 56*, 319–85.

Trahey, M., & White, L. (1993). Positive evidence and preemption in the second language classroom. *Studies in Second Language Acquisition, 15*, 181–204.

Trappes-Lomax, H. (2004). Discourse perspective. In A. Davies, & C. Elder (Eds.), *The handbook of applied linguistics* (pp. 133–64). Malden, MA: Blackwell.

Tsui, A. B. (2004). What teachers have always wanted to know-and how corpora can help. In J. Sinclair (Ed.), *How to use corpora in language teaching* (pp. 39–61). Amsterdam: John Benjamins.

Ueno, J. (2005). Grammar instruction and learning style. *Japanese Language and Literature, 39*, 1–25.

Ur, P. (1988). *Grammar practice activities: A practical guide for teachers*. Cambridge: Cambridge University Press.

Vaezi, S. (2006). Teaching foreign languages to children: From theory to practice. *ILI Language Teaching Journal, 2*, 43–55.

Vaipae, S. (2001). Language minority students in Japanese public schools. In M. Noguchi, & S. Fotos (Eds.), *Studies in Japanese bilingualism* (pp. 184–233). Clevedon: Multilingual Matters.

Van den Branden, K. (1997). Effects of negotiation on language learners' output. *Language Learning, 47*, 589–636.

VanPatten, B. (1993). Grammar teaching for the acquisition of rich classroom. *Foreign Language Annals, 26*, 435–50.

——(1996). *Input processing and grammar instruction in second language acquisition.* Norwood, NJ: Ablex.

——(2002a). Processing instruction: An update. *Language Learning, 52,* 755–803.

——(2002b). Processing the content of input-processing and processing instruction research: A response to Dekeyser, Salaberry, Robinson, and Harrington. *Language Learning, 52,* 825–31.

——(2004). Input processing in second language acquisition. In B. VanPatten (Ed.), *Processing instruction: Theory, research, and commentary* (pp. 5–31). Mahwah, NJ: Lawrence Erlbaum.

——(2009). Processing matters in input enhancement. In T. Piske, & M. Young-Scholten (Eds.), *Input matters in SLA* (pp. 47–61). Bristol: Multilingual Matters.

VanPatten, B., & Cadierno, T. (1993). Explicit instruction and input processing. *Studies in Second Language Acquisition, 15,* 225–44.

VanPatten, B., & Oikkenon, S. (1996). Explanation vs. structured input in processing instruction. *Studies in Second Language Acquisition, 18,* 495–510.

Vygotsky, L. S. (1978). *Mind in society: The development of higher psychological processes.* Cambridge, MA: Harvard University Press.

——(1986). *Thought and language.* Cambridge, MA: MIT Press.

Wajnryb, R. (1990). *Grammar dictation.* Oxford: Oxford University Press.

Warschauer, M. (2004). Technological change and the future of call. In S. Fotos, & C. Browne (Eds.), *New perspectives on call for second language classrooms* (pp. 15–26). Mahwah, NJ: Lawrence Erlbaum.

Weaver, C. (1996). *Teaching grammar in context.* Portsmouth, NH: Boynton/Cook Publishers.

Wertsch, J. V. (1985). *Vygotsky and the social formation of mind.* Cambridge, MA: Harvard University Press.

White, J. (1998). Getting the learners' attention: A typographical input enhancement study. In C. Doughty, & J. Williams (Eds.), *Focus on form in classroom second language acquisition* (pp. 85–113). Cambridge: Cambridge University Press.

White, L. (1991). Adverb placement in second language acquisition: Some effects of positive and negative evidence in the classroom. *Second Language Research, 7,* 133–61.

Widdowson, H. G. (1973). An applied linguistic approach to discourse analysis. Unpublished doctoral dissertation, University of Edinburgh.

——(1978). *Teaching language as communication.* Oxford: Oxford University Press.

——(1990). *Aspects of language teaching.* Oxford: Oxford University Press.

——(2003). *Defining issues in English language teaching.* Oxford: Oxford University Press.

Wilkins, D. (1976). *Notional syllabuses.* Oxford: Oxford University Press.

Williams, J. (2001). The effectiveness of spontaneous attention to form. *System, 29,* 325–40.

——(2005). Form-focused instruction. In E. Hinkel (Ed.), *Handbook on research in second language teaching and learning* (pp. 673–91). Mahwah, NJ: Lawrence Erlbaum Associates.

Williams, J., & Evans, J. (1998). What kind of focus and on which forms? In C. Doughty, & J. Williams (Eds.), *Focus on form in classroom second language acquisition* (pp. 139–55). Cambridge: Cambridge University Press.

Willis, D. (1996a). Accuracy, fluency and conformity. In J. Willis, & D. Willis (Eds.), *Challenge and change in language teaching* (pp. 44–51). Oxford: Heinemann.

——(1996b). Introduction. In J. Willis, & D. Willis (Eds.), *Challenge and change in language teaching* (pp. iv–vi). Oxford: Heinemann.

Willis, D., & Willis, J. (2007). *Doing task-based teaching.* Oxford: Oxford University Press.

Willis, J. (1996). A flexible framework for task-based learning. In J. Willis, & D. Willis (Eds.), *Challenge and change in language teaching* (pp. 52–62). Oxford: Heinemann.

Wong, W. (2005). *Input enhancement: From theory and research to the classroom.* New York: McGraw-Hill.

Woolard, G. (1999). *Grammar with laughter.* London: Language Teaching Publications.

Yuan, F. Y., & Ellis, R. (2003). The effects of pre-task planning and on-line planning on fluency, complexity and accuracy in L2 monologic oral production. *Applied Linguistics, 24,* 1–27.

Index